WELCOME to a unique program
from LOVE PRESS.

LoveLines:
The Honor Innovation™

That's right—*we work on an honor system.*

The retail value of this book is $6.95,
but you may take a copy without cost!
Would you just make a commitment to read the book
and share it with others if you enjoy it?

After that, *you're on your honor.*
If you believe in our message and ministry,
a financial gift of any amount
will be very appreciated.*
You may send a donation along with
the name of the LoveLiner™ location to:

LOVE PRESS
St. Luke's Building
P.O. Box 5000
Tarpon Springs, FL 34688-5000

*(Or you may use the postage-paid envelope
in the back of the book)*

*Contributions enable us to continue the LoveLines™ program.
A portion of the profit also goes to The Cataract Teaching Foundation to bring eye care to the poor in underdeveloped nations. When you send a donation to LOVE PRESS, please remember to let us know the name of the LoveLiner™ who made it possible for you to receive our book. We want to be sure to maintain accurate records. Would you write a note and tell us how you like the book, too? Thank you very much. Your response will encourage us a lot...

We're out to win your heart!™

The Dynamics of Worship

JAMES P. GILLS, M.D.

&

HEARTLIGHT

Other Books
by James P. Gills, M.D.
& HeartLight

Come Unto Me
Inspired by Dr. Gills' trip to the Holy Land, this book explores God's eternal desire for mankind to get to know Him intimately.

Temple Maintenance: Excellence, With Love
A how-to book for achieving total fitness of body, mind, and spirit.

The Unseen Essential: A Story For Our Troubled Times
A compelling, contemporary novel about one man's journey toward God's kind of love.

Your Smile Is Slipping!
Written in a light-hearted style with lots of cartoon illustrations to restore joy to your life.

Presents From Heaven
An inspiring guide to super fulfillment. . .God's way. Co-authored with psychotherapist and speaker, Dr. Tim Daley —scheduled for release in mid-1992.

All Scripture references are from the **New American Standard Bible,** The Lockman Foundation 1960, 1962, 1963, 1968, 1971, 1972, 1975, 1977. Thomas Nelson, Inc., Publishers. Used by permission.

The Dynamics of Worship
©1992 by James P. Gills, M.D.

Produced by HeartLight Creative Services

Published by LOVE PRESS:
A ministry of St Luke's Cataract and Laser Institute
Tarpon Springs, Florida
Printed in the United States of America
First edition: 100,000
Second edition: 100,000

ISBN 1-879938-03-0

To all who desire a deeper walk with the Lord.

With love.

To fall in love with God is the greatest of all romances.

To seek Him is the greatest of all adventures.

To find Him is the greatest human achievement.

—Author Unknown

Table of Contents

PART ONE: KINDLING

PART TWO: THE BLAZE BUILDS

Table of Contents

PART THREE: ALL- CONSUMING FIRE

APPENDIX 1 — BIBLIOGRAPHY

APPENDIX 2 — NOTES

About the Author

Foreword

Dr. Jim Gills' book on worship is a welcome resource to this field to which the Body of Christ is happily returning. I have enjoyed reading and rereading it and making it available to those I teach on praise and worship. The reader will find the presentation a delicate combination of concept and practice, technique and spirit, and knowledge and inspiration. The one who reads it is left with the sense that worship is the supreme recourse on planet earth and when exercised, becomes a supreme resource. Having studied extensively on this subject, I find ample cause to commend this fine work to any and all believers.

—Jack Taylor
Author: THE HALLELUJAH FACTOR

Acknowledgements

To Tom and Theo Boylan, the husband and wife writing/publishing team known as "HeartLight". . .who add intensity and creativity to my ideas and then carry through LOVE PRESS projects from beginning to end. They truly want to demonstrate a lifestyle of worship. That desire enables them to depend on the Lord in our work together. We make a good team. Thanks very much, HeartLight.

We all extend our appreciation to Drew Communications Group, Jacksonville, Florida, for typesetting, design assistance and printing: Randy Drew, *President;* John Rhymes, *Sales Manager;* Gary Goldsmith, *Creative Director;* Sheila Bole, *Typographer;* Serena Jacobs, *Quality Assurance Coordinator;* Preston Cannady, *Manager of Prepress;* Ray Pellum, *Pressroom Supervisor;* Chris Drew, *Production Assistant;* Bob Cooney, *Shipping and Inventory Clerk.* Great job, everyone!

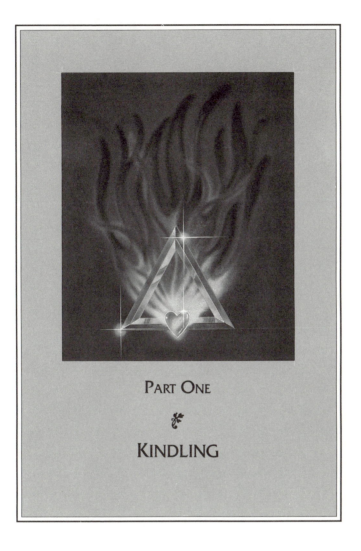

PART ONE

KINDLING

Chapter One

Prelude To Worship

INTER.
Biting winds whistled through the deserted streets of a quaint, northern town. The temperature continued to drop, but that failed to deter one lone man from venturing outside. Heavily bundled to protect himself against the sub-zero weather, with the ends of his plaid, woolen neck scarf flapping in the wind, Jake Matthews walked with steady, brisk strides. His hunched shoulders and forward lean gave him the appearance of a man on a mission. Who else would be out on such a fearsome night?

As Jake pressed onward to a destination known only to himself, he spotted a trembling, emaciated dog cowering for shelter behind a telephone pole. Something drew him a step closer. He couldn't be sure, but it looked like a child had played a cruel prank on the poor dog.

Jake squinted. Sure enough, a tin can was tied to the dog's tail and the rope was wrapped around the pole several times. In his frantic struggles to get free from the can, he must have run back and forth from pole to tree. All to no avail. Finally, with one last desperate dash in a circle, the animal had sealed his fate. Without a break in the weather, which was unlikely, he would make his last stand entangled around the telephone pole.

What a sorry sight! Jake thought as he stared at the dog. Compassion tugged at his heart. For the moment, he forgot how cold he was. Drawing closer still, he paused and inspected the creature. *He's skinny, all right. Looks miserable. Bald patches in his coat. A stray, no doubt. . .*

Jake stooped down, reached out his hand and called to the dog. Suspicious at first, and for good reason, the dog overcame his fears and gradually approached. Inch by slow inch he crept forward, whining with each step. Gently, Jake reached out his hand and stroked the frightened animal, all the while speaking kind words. After removing the string and tin can from his tail, the man lifted the dog up, opened his overcoat and tucked the bedraggled animal inside for the journey back home.

They arrived at last. As Jake went into the house, he explained to his wife how he found the half-starved little dog on the street. He urged her, "Please, sweetheart, put a blanket in the corner of the kitchen, by the heater where it's warm. We'll take care of him, at least for tonight." He looked down and shook his head. "He would've died if I'd left him out in the cold."

Mary smiled to herself, knowing her husband's soft heart for strays. One night would never be enough. She returned with a suitable blanket and together they lovingly placed the still-quivering creature upon it. He whimpered softly. They offered a delicious bowl of warm milk and bread, followed by some scraps from the evening meal. The famished dog devoured the feast. For the first time in many months, he wagged his tail (with caution) for the unusual kindness bestowed on him.

The next day, as Jake and Mary awoke to the early morning sunlight, the dog greeted his benefactors with a slightly more enthusiastic wag of his tail. As the couple exchanged a quick glance, they reached a decision. The dog, though not much to look at in his present state, had found a home.

"What should we name him, dear?" Jake asked. "He must have a name if he's to be part of the family." They were both silent for a few moments, then stared at the dog and at each other.

Mary volunteered with a chuckle, "The way he looks. . .*Old Bones* might suit him fine."

"True, he's not much of a prize right now," he answered. "You just wait, though! In a month or so he'll look like he's got royal blood in him." He paused and thought a moment. "How about *Monarch* for a name? Rather regal-sounding, don't you think? Besides, that's the name of a butterfly. You know how different *they* look from the caterpillar that spins a cocoon!"

Monarch he became.

Days and weeks passed since the new addition to the family. Time revealed an incredible metamorphosis taking place in the old dog. His eyes became clearer, his nose grew cool and moist, and his tail wagged vigorously whenever anyone even glanced his way. More remarkable, though, was his coat. The silky, russet-colored fur glistened in the sunlight streaming in through the window onto his favorite napping spot. What a change in Monarch! After lots of good food and tender loving care, Jake and Mary could scarcely recognize the fine-looking animal as the same miserable stray of four weeks ago.

Each afternoon about four-thirty, Monarch whined and scratched at the door to go outside. He trotted to the end of the walk, sat by the gate and waited for his master to come home from work. The sound of the family car coming up the street was etched clearly in his memory. As soon as the familiar noise reached his ears, he would begin barking excitedly and thumping his tail with wild abandon.

Joy. . .JOY! Master was home!

Then, when Monarch heard the car door slam shut, he could restrain himself no longer. He ran in circles and bounded about, almost knocking over his beloved Jake as he came through the gate. From that moment on, master and dog remained inseparable for the rest of the evening.

One night after dinner Jake was snoozing in his favorite easy chair with his arm dangling over the arm rest. Monarch lay nearby in utter bliss. Suddenly, Jake awakened to something wet nuzzling his hand. As he leaned over the side of the chair, his gaze met two of the most loving eyes any dog ever had for his master. He nodded and smiled as, over and over, Monarch licked the hand of the one to whom he owed his very life. It was the same hand, in fact, that had reached out to him in far different circumstances.

Above all else, one thing stood out in the scene. It was obvious that Monarch had followed Jake into the room and had lain by his side out of sheer devotion. He didn't beg for food or whine for attention, but merely expressed gratitude for being able to rest in his master's presence. Looking up with eyes filled with rapt adoration, and as the best way of expressing the love he felt—licking the hand of his master—Monarch was content (based on a story by A.P. Gibbs).[1]

We humans have a lot to learn from old Monarch. I do. He shows us how to worship! God longs for each of His children to express such love for Him. And why shouldn't we? Not one of us can ever come to our Master on our own terms. Or by our own merits. We have one claim to fame: without God, Satan's chains bind us tight around the post of sin. We deserve only the wrath of a holy, righteous God but instead, He reaches down to us with His ultimate expression of love.

Monarch differs from most of us in that *he knew* his master had saved his life on that bitter winter night. His response in return? Show his feelings of love without hesitation or reservation. Monarch's response is not mere fiction. Most dogs act the very same towards their owners. Consider the following true saga written long after Monarch's story.

Best-selling author and psychologist Dr. James Dobson, in his March, 1991, newsletter, tells about how the family acquired their new dog, Mitzi. While mourning the loss of Mindy, their twelve-year-old yellow labrador, they began searching for another pet to fill the empty spot she left in their home. They scouted around the local animal shelter for the most pathetic, least likely adoption candidate. One nobody else would want. It wasn't a hard task.

A twelve-week-old semi-starved pup with pneumonia, a barely healing broken jaw, and a bad case of worms trembled at the back of her cage. She stole their hearts with a single hug. Not too long afterward, the Dobson's daughter went back to the shelter to pick her up. Dr. Dobson describes their puppy one month later, "I wish you could see Mitzi today. She is fat, healthy and deliriously happy. When I get home at night, she romps to the front door like a buffalo in a stampede. It is as though she knows we rescued her from a living death."

Notice any similarities between Mitzi and Monarch? Besides their dismal pasts, I mean. Think about their love for their rescuers. Both dogs were so spontaneous. Uninhibited. Enthusiastic! We human beings find it far more difficult to adore our Master who saved us. Worship often involves a life-long process of learning to simply "let go." One popular worship song speaks of having a spirit set free for worship. I'm still in the process, believe me.

How *do* we cultivate an attitude of gratitude towards God? We'll cover that, so stay with me. By the last page, I believe you'll not only know how, but you will be doing it. Our goal for *The Dynamics of Worship* is to make each of us more like Monarch and Mitzi and less like our natural selves—where our relationship to God is concerned, that is. We'll be addressing six major aspects of worship throughout the book (but not necessarily in this strict order).

1. *Who* we worship (Does He really deserve it?)
2. *What* worship is (And what it isn't)
3. *Where* we worship (Does it matter?)
4. *When* to worship (How about non-stop?)
5. *Why* we should worship (Plenty of reasons)
6. *How* we worship (That's a "hot" topic!)

So let's begin by reminding ourselves why God created us in the first place. We have a deep, inner craving in us that He alone can fill. In fact, He created us to love Him,

> Now we were made to worship. . . All else fulfills its design; flowers are still fragrant and lilies are still beautiful and the bees still search for nectar amongst the flowers; the birds still sing with their thousand-voice choir on a summer's day, and the sun and the moon and the stars all move on their rounds doing the will of God.
>
> And from what we can learn from the Scriptures we believe that the seraphim and cherubim and powers and dominions are still fulfilling their design—worshipping God who also created them and breathed into them the breath of life. Man alone sulks in his cave. Man alone, with all of his brilliant intelligence, with all of his amazing, indescribable and wonderful equipment, still sulks in his cave.[2]

How few people understand and accept man's intrinsic need to worship God! Only as we acknowledge the emptiness that cries for worship, can the constant unrest within us be settled. Our search for God will be most meaningful when we realize the utter barrenness of a soul separated from Him.

The void within us is spiritual. Yet, how often do we look to other areas of life in hope of finding the answer to our malaise? Everyone has heard stories of the busy executive, ruthlessly driven to success after success, but who never achieves fulfillment. How about the "supermom" who loses herself in her children—only to feel devastated by loneliness when they grow up and move out their own? More often than not, these unbalanced lifestyles stem from an unrecognized, or purposely avoided, spiritual longing. They want to love God, but don't know it.

In varying degrees, most of us are probably guilty of seeking satisfaction through either intellectual, emotional, or physical stimulation. *Futility, futility, futility*...moaned King Solomon after he had sampled every diversion known to man. It's an age-old problem. The glitter of earth-bound methods loses its sparkle, leaving us disillusioned and depressed. (I ran down that dead-end street for years.) Sadly enough, even after many people *know* that the living God is *the source* of contentment, some still refuse to allow Him to do what He desires in their lives.

There once was in man a true happiness of which now remains to him only the mark and empty trace, which he in vain tries to fill from all his surroundings, seeking from things absent the help he does not obtain in things present. But these are all inadequate, because the infinite abyss can only be filled by an infinite and immutable object, that is to say, only by God Himself.[3]

In our avoidance of God, we find ourselves surrounded by much company throughout history. When we look to the children of Israel as our spiritual predecessors, we see them running from their Creator at Mt. Sinai. After God freed His people from Egyptian slavery with one mighty miracle after another, He made them a most amazing offer. He asked them to enter into a personal relationship with Him. Listen to God's words to Moses (for him to pass on to the Israelites),

" 'You yourselves have seen what I did to the Egyptians, and how I bore you on eagles' wings, and brought you to Myself. Now then, if you will indeed obey My voice and keep My covenant, then you shall be My own possession among all the peoples, for all the earth is Mine; and you shall be to Me a kingdom of priests and a holy nation.' These are the words that you shall speak to the sons of Israel."

Exodus 19:4-6

Note the Israelites' enthusiastic response,

> And all the people perceived the thunder and
> the lightning flashes and the sound of the trumpet
> and the mountain smoking; and when the people saw
> it, they trembled and stood at a distance. Then they
> said to Moses, "Speak to us yourself and we will listen;
> but let not God speak to us, lest we die." And Moses
> said to the people, "Do not be afraid; for God has
> come in order to test you, and in order that the fear
> of Him may remain with you, so that you may not sin."
>
> Exodus 20:18-20

The people failed to grasp the significance of God's invitation. He was offering them the answer to their deep longing, but because of fear and misunderstanding, they preferred to remain far from Him.

Centuries after the Mt. Sinai experience, neither the offer nor the response had changed. Jesus was engaged in a candid, yet compassionate, conversation with a woman of Samaria. Alongside a well, He was extending the well-spring of abundant life to her. He knew sexual promiscuity could no more fill the needy vacuum within her, than could mere obedience of the law for the Israelites. "No man can meet a woman's spiritual needs, and a woman has not been born who can meet a man's spiritual needs. Our spirit belongs to God and can only find fulfillment and complete satisfaction in Him."[4]

The woman at the well failed to see her inner poverty and asked Jesus, instead, about the proper *place* to worship. Wasn't she evading the real issue—letting God get close to her? If we'll admit it, we run from Him today just like she and the Israelites did. We do so in the name of "religion." Not worship. Malcolm Smith, the British teacher, helps us smile at our ancestors' standoffish attitude (and our own) in his excellent three-tape series, "How to Rise Above Burnout."

❧

You understand why religion was invented. It was to keep God at a safe distance. I used to believe that all the religions of the world were men reaching out for God. It isn't. All the religions of the world are there to keep God at a safe distance. You see, man knows there's a God, but he's scared spitless of Him, so he's got to keep Him away.

So I know what we'll do...we'll build a God-house and put Him in there! So we have the "house of God." That's got Him off my back. If He's in *His* house, He's not in mine! We'll give Him a certain day. That's it, we'll give Him one day. That gives me six.

I'll give Him times. We'll have hours of prayer. That means I won't have to pray all the time. Religion says, "Spend fifteen minutes in prayer every day." That gets Him off your back. Fifteen minutes. You've got the other twenty-three and three quarters. Right? Keep Him at a distance. See, I know He's there, but keep Him at a distance.

I tell you what we'll do...we'll employ people full-time to talk to Him. Then *I* don't have to, see. Religion. All religion is like that. I'm not joking. Religion keeps God at arm's length from man. And now religion is uneasy. Why? Because the God they're supposed to represent has *really* turned up among them. And they're very upset. God has escaped! He got out of the house! And He's walking among them, and He doesn't fit at all what they thought He was like.[5]

Genuine worship frees us from the bondage of pre-conceived notions and fake religion. Only as we worship, our spirits having been "released from captivity to soar in the presence of God," (Cornwall) can the "quiet desperation," as Thoreau called it, be relieved. No wonder Thoreau felt desperate. His writings express the humanistic belief in *selfhood*

❦

reigning supreme. (Nature is up there near the top of his list, too.) His ideas provided him no opportunity to worship Someone outside himself—the eternal Creator—the God of the Bible. Our answer to fulfillment lies not in man or in nature, which are both God's handiwork, but with the Lord of glory Himself. And in our worship of Him.

> Worship is written upon the heart of man by the hand of God...In a broad sense, worship is inseparable from and is an expression of life. It is not that man cannot live without worship, it is that he cannot *fully* live without worship...man was made to worship as surely as he was made to breathe. We may restrict the expression of worship for a season, just as we may briefly hold our breath, but there is an inward craving for worship that cannot be permanently stilled.[6]

Even for the most dedicated Christian, today's world of push-button conveniences and fast food chains can be challenging to our spiritual priorities. Yet, we've got to get free of the influence of these easy-come, easy-go habits if we are to develop a balanced love relationship with God. There are no shortcuts, that I know of. But I have found some keys that will unlock the door to true worship and kindle within each of us *a heart aflame.* We'll be exploring those ideas in more depth throughout this book.

How would you describe your own walk with God? Be honest with yourself. Could you say that you're enthusiastic? Alive and filled with His power? Are you consumed with zeal? Do you glow with a burning desire to please Him? Can you, like Monarch, rest contentedly in your Master's presence—and just enjoy *being with Him?* These questions measure the heart-fire of love. Perhaps the flame is but dying embers at this point in your life, or has even gone out altogether. If so, you might consider a statement by the late A. W. Tozer: *"Worship* is the missing jewel of the evangelical church!"[7]

❦

Many Christians have begun to discover the inadequacy of mere knowledge of God through His Word. Or even of their dedication to Him. They may have practiced both of these concepts from their youth, and yet, much to their dismay, admit that their hearts remain stone cold towards God. They don't love Him at all. Something is missing—the zeal, the passion that marks a true worshipper.

A mature relationship with the Lord embodies three components: *knowledge* of Him, *covenant* with Him, and *worship* of Him. These elements represent the *complete* love of God. If the relationship is to grow in a healthy manner, they must be present in equal measure. The three enhance one another in a kind of divine synergy. From worship comes an expansion of intimate knowledge and covenant, which in turn reinforces worship even further. Each element complements and completes the other two, but worship kindles the fire of passion for God (more about this in chapter two).

In my own personal search for worship, I attended many a Sunday service, crammed significant amounts of Bible verses in my head, but failed to experience worship in my heart. Even in the Holy Land I found meaningful *places* to worship. Yet, I still lacked the ability to do so with any gusto or sincerity. Finally, in my attempts to catch this elusive butterfly, I realized that the fault lay not in the geographic location. The responsibility rested squarely in my lap. I had to admit to God and to myself that I really did not know *how* to worship. For years I longed for the answer to this question to fill the hunger inside me. I searched in many ways, some a little unusual.

"What is worship, anyway?" I wondered. I had picked a difficult question because worship involves nearly every aspect of life. As a starting point, we can investigate the Hebrew word *shachah* translated "worship" in the Old Testament. It means to lower one's body, or stretch out with one's face to the ground as a means of paying honor, to bow, humbly ask in earnest, do obeisance, or to show reverence. We worship something when we pay it great respect, when we consider it extremely precious, enough to adore. In the New Testament, the word for worship, *proskuneo,* means to kiss, (as a dog would lick his master's hand); to bow down or crouch closer to, literally or figuratively, to lie flat before someone to show reverence, respect and adoration.

Judson Cornwall draws a contrast between the meaning of the Old and New Testament words for worship. The two terms actually describe the difference between the old and new covenants. (Remember the Israelites cringing in fear at a safe distance from Mt. Sinai while Moses talked with God?) Judson makes it clear when he writes,

> The word "proskuneo" is far more descriptive than the Hebrew word "shachah," for to the bowing is added kissing, and this requires close contact. We can bow at a distance, but kissing requires contact.[8]

Webster's dictionary sheds more light on the subject of worship: "paying divine honor to God: a feeling of respect and a reverence for power, position, merit and virtue; dignity, worth, obsequious devotion and paying divine honor."

These definitions address the external actions that may accompany worship, but speak little about what is actually taking place in the heart. A few other sources may help to broaden our understanding of this all-important activity. For example, "The chief end and duty of man is to glorify God and enjoy Him forever," states the Westminster Catechism. That sums up worship quite well. *Glorify. Enjoy.*

Someone else described worship as "a romance with God, an idealistic adventure of the extravagant and the mysterious in the spiritual realm." How poetic, but true! In his writings, A. W. Tozer approached worship as "a feeling in the heart, expressed in an appropriate way." He also stated that the "soul of the worshipper should be the most godlike thing in the universe."[9]

William Temple, the late Archbishop of Canterbury, gave a beautiful description of worship in his book, *The Hope of a New World,*

> To worship is to quicken the conscience by the
> holiness of God, to feed the mind with the truth of
> God, to purge the imagination by the beauty of God,
> to open the heart to the love of God, to devote the
> will to the purpose of God.[10]

Worship means to "practice the presence of God" in
everything we do, every time we do it. Brother Lawrence, a
seventeenth-century French Carmelite monk, wrote an entire
book about the subject that has retained popularity until now.
To practice the presence of God we must become intimately
involved with the person of Jesus Christ. The special relationship
and corresponding closeness that develop through the act of
worship produce an obedience not possible in our own strength.

Granted, such lofty worship challenges us to the utmost,
but the effect proves to be electrifying and fulfilling. That author
I mentioned was right—worship *is* no less than a "romance"
with God! All we need is a revelation of our Savior's mental and
spiritual anxiety in Gethsemane...His fateful walk to
Calvary...the agony He endured on the cross...and yet, His
triumphant resurrection. One would think we'd shout, "Hallelujah! No *wonder* they call Him the Savior!" (The last sentence
is the title of a fantastic book by Max Lucado.)

So worship, then, is a joining with, and a rejoicing in, all
that God is...all that He's done...and all that He's yet to do.
How can we fail to respond with grateful adoration? How can
we sit on our hands? I don't know, but we do. Every day.

Worship consists of a feeling in the heart stemming from
the "humbling but delightful sense of admiring awe and
astonishing wonder of the God of the universe."[11] A worshipper experiences motivational feelings, and yes, he has to express
these feelings. Without emotion there can be no true worship.

But being an occasional worshipper "when the mood
strikes" falls far short of attaining a lifestyle of worship—the key
to spiritual transformation. John MacArthur, Jr.'s words speak
volumes, "Worship is not merely an activity to be injected into

our schedules at certain intervals; rather, worship is itself a whole-life commitment, an all-encompassing response to Holy God. . ."[12]

If worship is love responding to love, and if nothing in heaven, on earth, or in hell can separate us from God's love, then surely nothing can separate us from responding to that love. That response is worship.[13]

FIRE-SEEKER'S COMPANION
Questions for Group Interaction or Individual Reflection

1. Compare and contrast yourself with Monarch and Mitzi. Do you really need and want profound changes in your life?

2. Why did God create you? Have you fulfilled that purpose? What effect has that had on you?

3. How have human beings responded to God over the centuries? Why?

4. Has the twentieth-century lifestyle affected your ability to worship? How and why? What can you do about it?

5. What part does worship play in a balanced love of God? Name the other two important components.

6. Give as many definitions of worship as you can. Which mean the most to you? Why?

7. Why do you want to be a worshipper?

OPEN SHARING: FEEL FREE TO DISCUSS QUESTIONS OR ANYTHING RELATED TO THE CHAPTER THAT MINISTERED TO MEMBERS OF THE GROUP. LET THE HOLY SPIRIT LEAD YOU.

FIRE-STARTER'S PREPARATION
("Lab" Exercise)

SPEND TIME ALONE AND TOGETHER WORSHIPPING THE LORD. BEFORE AND AFTER, RECORD YOUR THOUGHTS AND FEELINGS IN A JOURNAL. WRITE DOWN CHANGES YOU NOTICE IN YOUR LIFE.

NOTES

Chapter Two

A Delicate Balance

 nowledge. Covenant. Worship. Three vital elements that comprise an ideal relationship between creation and Creator. No one element carries more weight than either of the other two; rather, the three support one another in a beautiful symmetry. Three of anything means a good, solid amount. Some people say three is a perfect number, especially in light of the divine trinity—Father, Son, and Holy Spirit. Out of twelve disciples, Jesus chose just three men, Peter, James and John, to be closest to Him. After three days, He rose from the dead. Why not two days? Or four? We can't be sure. We only know He completed the Father's work in that time.

Three represents special strength. The Bible tells us in Ecclesiastes that a cord of three strands (symbolic of a marriage with Christ in the center) holds together best. Geometry teaches that a three-sided shape can endure stress more than other shapes. Hence, engineers often design bridges utilizing steel structures in a triangular pattern.

Have you ever heard about the main difference between two carbon compounds—diamonds and graphite (pencil lead)? Of course, everyone knows a diamond is the hardest stone, graphite, quite soft. The reason is this: in a diamond, the arrangement of carbon atoms forms a rigid, three-dimensional network instead of a flat plane! Recognizing, then, the "value of three" principle, let's take a look again at what I believe makes up an ideal relationship with God:

Knowledge.

Covenant.

Worship.

The symbol for such a perfect union? *A triangle, of course!*

As an aid to a better grasp of this concept of the human-divine relationship, we'll use an adaptation of psychologist Stern-berg's love triangles. He believes *intimacy, commitment* and *passion* make up relationships between two people. We can expand that to *knowledge, covenant* and *worship* in our relationship with God. The following illustrations show that it takes balance to achieve the highest possible love.

Every interaction that a person experiences has, to one

degree or another, the following components: *emotional* (knowledge/intimacy), *cognizant* (covenant/commitment), and *motivational* (worship/passion) factors. Each plays a vital part.

The outer triangle portrays the ideal balance between *knowledge, covenant* and *worship* in a relationship with God, while the inner shows a corresponding balance between *intimacy, commitment* and *passion* in a marital relationship, for example. Harmony in either union should be our goal if we want to develop a healthy love that will grow, endure and produce lasting fruit. Let's look at the marriage triangle first. What do we mean by *intimacy? Commitment? Passion?*

Intimacy

On the emotional side of the love triangle lies intimacy, or "knowing"—a term that holds much more significance in the original biblical languages. In both Hebrew and Greek, "to know" implies an intimate relationship best seen in a very close friendship. To understand a spouse in this manner does not come easily. It takes time, effort and sharing many different ideas and experiences. As one soul opens up to another, comradeship and mutual dependence lend support during times of trouble.

Many people who have been divorced, in looking back at the factors that may have led to their break-ups, realize that emotional intimacy had diminished gradually as the years drifted by. They made the mistake of not pursuing a close friendship with their mates. As they grew in separate directions, they communicated less, shared fewer interests, and finally divorced with nothing in common.

Commitment

Now for the cognizant side of the love triangle. That's the "down-to-brass-tacks" loyalty in a marital relationship. It develops on more of a straightforward course than either intimacy or passion, and provides the reliable strength necessary for the relationship to survive all the ups and downs of life.

Commitment will grow or wither depending on how it is nurtured. Each spouse makes a vow to do whatever possible to ensure the success of the marriage. That means total fidelity. No allowances for casual sexual encounters of any kind. What a solid foundation of trust that it provides! Another classic example of commitment exists in the relationship between parent and child. Regardless of what the child does, the parents' commitment never falters. Well, almost never.

The following saying from a framed print hanging in our home describes this consistent quality better than I can:

Commitment is what transforms a promise into reality.
It is the words that speak boldly of your intentions
And the actions which speak louder than words.
It is making the time. . .when there is none.
Coming through time after time, year after year.
Commitment is the stuff character is made of;
the power to change the face of things.
It is the daily triumph of integrity over skepticism.
                                              —Author Unknown

Passion

On the motivational side of the triangle we find the passion level in a relationship. Romance and physical union between husband and wife are essential components for fulfilling love. When they become "one flesh" in tender passion, their relationship embraces a uniqueness they have with no one else. Passion motivates them to greater commitment and leads to deeper intimacy with their partner. Passion cements the whole relationship into one cohesive bond. Trust grows during those moments, and they are able to express feelings otherwise unapproachable.

Marriages based *entirely* on the passionate aspect, however, often encounter difficulties that spell disaster. These relationships are characterized by numerous partners, varying interests, loose living and consistently high rates of divorce. The volatile nature of passion causes "love" to flare up, but having no solid core, the relationship dies out.

A counterfeit of marital passion lies at the heart of those high-school crushes and childhood infatuations we've all experienced. Consider the schoolboy who "falls in love" with a beautiful girl in one of his classes. Although he thinks about her constantly, he never quite musters enough courage to introduce himself and get to know her better. Contrary to this, passion between spouses should be based on emotional intimacy, plus a devoted commitment that encourages them to "hang in there" when the going gets tough.

From the Human to the Divine

Ideally, every relationship would remain perfectly balanced. We live in a not-so-ideal world, however, with less-than-perfect human beings. Fortunately, we serve a perfect God who delights in a *just balance.*

By drawing a comparison between various interpersonal relationships and the human love of God, we'll be better able to understand the role of worship in spirituality. Intimacy/knowledge, commitment/covenant, and passion/worship will be present in varying degrees and change from time to time. In this section we'll look at the off-balance combinations of these three elements that occur most often. An equilateral triangle (three equal sides) illustrates the model relationship. Scalene and isosceles triangles represent imbalances.

Acquaintances make up the majority of our interpersonal encounters. They exhibit a noticeable lack of *any* of the three elements of love, as shown by the dotted lines in the triangle. A man who communtes on a train to work every morning may

exchange greetings and small talk with other commuters, but this is the extent of their relationship. Many people never develop more than casual acquaintances. At the root may lurk psychological problems, such as feelings of inferiority and fear of rejection.

How about someone acquainted with God? This person *knows about* the God of creation but certainly doesn't love Him. He and God have bumped into each other now and then. The person may have even joined a local church and sung hymns with the congregation, but he doesn't have a relationship with the Lord. His is merely an *awareness* of Someone he doesn't know on an intimate basis. No covenant and no worship, either.

Ice-Cold Relationships

Brrrr! This variation of human relationships boasts strong commitment, but has so little intimacy and passion, it sends shivers down the spine. If marriage partners restrict the flow of genuine friendship and physical closeness between them, they end up with a relationship whose strength lies solely in the existence of the institution of marriage itself. It exists; therefore, it will continue to exist. The "until death do us part" flag flies alone at half-mast in bleak skies of marital unhappiness. Prearranged marriages often feel the chill, as well as unions where couples have thrown a wet blanket on the fire of passion.

In inspecting a cold relationship with God, we notice one important fact. Regardless of varying levels of knowledge and covenant, worship remains at an all-time low. Imbalance occurs for many reasons, primarily because of cultural or doctrinal restraints. Far too common today is the frigid church who can't worship the God she serves. Even sadder is the church that once

experienced glorious worship, but has lost her ability to express love to God. Consider the Lord's words to the church at Ephesus, *"But I have this against you, that you have left your first love"* (Revelation 2:4).

A cold spiritual relationship may develop along several lines. The first example shows an abundance of covenant, some knowledge, and minimal worship. People here are often quite committed to the *habit* of their religion, but don't really know what they believe or why they believe it. Strong commitment does have a benefit, however. These churches may have developed a ritual that will hold them together if all else fails. The trouble is, they mistake formalized behavior for true worship. In those cases where worship has declined to ritual, the Lord issues a stern warning. He will take away the light of His presence,

"Remember therefore from where you have fallen, and repent and do the deeds you did at first; or else I am coming to you, and will remove your lampstand out of its place—unless you repent."
Revelation 2:5

The next example shows a better balance between knowledge and covenant, but still leaves worship at a minimum. God's heart of compassion has yet to thaw the ice enough to kindle in the church-goers *a heart aflame.* They know what they should do based on the Word, and they're committed enough to try to act on that knowledge. Bible studies and service-oriented projects may even flourish in these cold churches, but without the fire of worship to give motivation and burn up impurities, judgmentalism and criticism tarnish relationships. Heart-felt joy is missing.

In the third cold variation upon a theme, knowledge has become the predominant factor. Intellectuals who study the Word of God, but have less-than-optimum covenant and again, minimal worship, typify these chilly churches. For instance, cold Christians may look down on those who lack the same level of Bible knowledge or who fall short on memory verses.

Chasing after the rabbit of knowledge for knowledge's sake alone leads right into the briar patch of legalism and self-righteous piety. Jesus often addressed two well-known religious groups, the Scribes and Pharisees. They had a corner on the religiosity market.

He showed disdain for their intellectual assent and external shows of obedience. "White-washed tombs," He called them and pointed out how they resembled persons who washed the outside of a cup and left the inside dirty. The same goes for us. Without internal obedience of the heart encouraged through worship, the result may be a Christian who, in addition to being cold, is disobedient to God's laws.

Luke-Warm Relationships

As comfortable as a pair of old kick-around shoes, the warm relationship between two people sports a high level of intimacy. For strength, this situation relies on shared emotional experiences and the results they produce. Daily routine and significant events, even tragic ones, bring about closeness and mutual acceptance that lend support to each spouse.

Warm mates exchange thoughts and ideas, and so improve their communication. They begin to know more about one another than anybody else. "Best buddies," we could call them—those who enjoy a companionship that endures even after physical attraction has faded. Passion plays an insignificant role in these relationships, often to the disappointment of one partner. Commitment may be present, and may even verge on unhealthy, emotional co-dependency. They "need" each other's constant approval to feel good about themselves, but at the same time, take each other for granted. Mutual boredom puts them to sleep.

How about a warm love of God relationship with some Bible knowledge, some covenant and a measure of worship? Christians in this category have been reading the Bible for awhile, can recognize many verses, but fail to grow in worship. They know God through His Word and may even have a degree of friendship with Him, but their hearts are not ablaze with zeal. His holy majesty doesn't faze them a whole lot. They think they're on pretty good terms with "the

man upstairs," no matter how they act. It's a cozy situation for them, they feel. God's stern warning about lukewarm Christianity can light a fire under the complacent saint, *"So because you are lukewarm, and neither hot nor cold, I will spit you out of My mouth"* (Revelation 3:16).

Red-Hot Relationships

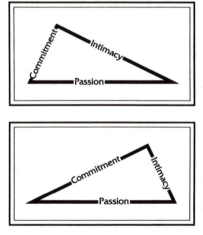

Hot relationships between people sizzle with passion. When passion as the strongest ingredient teams up with intimacy, a form of intense romantic love emerges. This "Romeo and Juliet" kind of love stirs up many young adults into a summer affair—until the first bout of disillusionment.

A second form of hot love occurs when passion and commitment are very strong, but intimacy is missing. Sternberg labeled this "Hollywood love." Here, the heat of fulfilling passion alone forges commitment, so the relationship lacks any emotional core necessary to endure the test of time.

Wild pendulum swings characterize hot relationships. The cycle begins on a very positive note and then veers in the opposite direction. This period of on-again, off-again, or hot-cold, usually continues for a brief time. If it persists, it develops a highly negative factor. What began in the heat of passion winds up on the ice of contempt.

I don't intend to downgrade passion, by any means. Hugging, kissing and making love within the bonds of marriage keep the home fires burning. In proper balance and at the appropriate time, physical affection enhances the desire for renewed commitment and even greater intimacy.

Hot relationships occur also in the love of God, with similar inherent weaknesses. Notice the example representing excessive worship with little emphasis placed on the Word—and the necessary obedience to it.

Christians who have this kind of relationship with the Lord go to church to experience an emotional "high" from congregational worship. If their private times with God don't include some fantastic supernatural visions as well, they think He has left them. They fail to recognize the volatility of trying to live from one "spiritual fix" to the next. Like any addiction, artificial worship creates an unhealthy dependence in the devotee.

In another variation of the hot relationship, the level of knowledge approaches the degree of worship, but a covenant relationship with God has not been firmly established. Churches of this nature may experience glorious worship. Members love to chew on the meat of divine revelation from the pulpit instead of spiritual "baby food" they think other Christians get. But they can't seem to make the transition from the mountaintop of academic knowledge to the trenches of dedicated service. During the heat of battle, they fall out, exhausted.

Without the deep commitment involved in covenant, endurance qualities of faith and trust become meaningless. When carried to extremes, lack of covenant may even lead to doubting the deity of God during rough times. Hot fellowships ride out many up and down swells in total membership rolls, and they hold a special attraction for Christians who have left other churches for one reason or another. Even in those cases of church growth explosion, a high rate of instability threatens to undermine progress.

Fired-up Christians who frequent these churches often exhibit a similar lack of commitment in their personal lives. When marital problems arise, they may be more apt to seek divorce. Their overall work and personal habits turn out to be far less than optimum. These vibrant, outgoing Christians know God and sincerely love to worship Him. Unfortunately, they fall short on a long-term commitment to obedience.

The third example of a hot relationship with God lacks knowledge. These churches, and the people who frequent them, have perhaps made a covenant with a God they love to worship. They just don't know Him very well yet.

Because of their lack of knowledge of the Word, these Christians have a hard time sensing direction from the Holy Spirit of God. Their fervor to enjoy Him puts them in danger of being led astray. A Word deficiency may allow the zealous and hungry, but uneducated, Christian to wander along aberrant paths— even into cults.

Knowledge of God's Word maintains the accuracy of our *worship,* while *covenant* keeps us going over the long haul. All facets of the love relationship play a vital role. John Piper expressed balance so well in his book, **Desiring God,**

> Truth without emotion produces dead orthodoxy and a church full (or half-full) of artificial admirers (like people who write generic anniversary cards for a living). On the other hand, emotion without truth produces empty frenzy and cultivates shallow people who refuse the discipline of rigorous thought. But true worship comes from people who are deeply emotional and who love deep and sound doctrine. Strong affections for God rooted in truth are the bone and marrow of Biblical worship.[14]

Achieving and maintaining balance enables our love to evolve into all that God planned for us. Of supreme importance, of course, is the relationship we develop with the Father through Jesus Christ. Christian activity will only be as fulfilling and fruitful as the union we have with Jesus. We'll tackle that subject in the next few chapters.

Now mull over the late A.W. Tozer's famous statement again: "Worship is the missing jewel of the evangelical church." Which triangle best applies? Hint: a "cold" one. It would be the triangle with two long sides being fairly equal in knowledge and covenant, but with minimal worship. I would venture to say that chilly churches outrank overheated ones, especially in the United States. Many people believe the lack of fervent worship has caused Christian churches everywhere to head into a dizzying downward spiral in membership, despite high levels of covenant and knowledge. The *motivational* component has been voted out of the curriculum by stuffy saints!

Maybe you, too, want to do something to help bring passionate worship back to the church. Stay with us for the rest of this book. Like enthusiastic diamond miners on an expedition to South Africa, let's set out in search of this precious gem. Once found, we can restore worship's rightful place—adorning the Bride of Christ with sparkling beauty.

Balance is our goal!

FIRE-SEEKER'S COMPANION
Questions for Group Interaction
or Individual Reflection

1. Name three key elements of a relationship between spouses and then, between you and the Lord. Which element is cognizant, which emotional, which motivational? Draw a triangle representing the ideal, balanced relationship.

2. Think about the advantages and disadvantages of acquaintances versus relationships. Which do you have with your spouse (if you're married) and with the Lord? Why?

3. What three major "categories" of relationships did you study in this chapter? Where do you fit best as an individual? How about your church?

4. Talk about the characteristics of various "cold" relationships—human and divine. What dangers lie in these conditions? Draw triangles to represent them.

5. How about warm relationships? What advantages or disadvantages do you notice? Draw a triangle that indicates the imbalance.

6. Hot relationships come next. Describe them. Any cautions to watch out for? Draw the various triangles.

7. What similarities and differences do you see between marital relationships and a Christian's love for God? Explain.

OPEN SHARING: FEEL FREE TO DISCUSS QUESTIONS OR ANYTHING RELATED TO THE CHAPTER THAT MINISTERED TO MEMBERS OF THE GROUP. LET THE HOLY SPIRIT LEAD YOU.

FIRE-STARTER'S PREPARATION
("Lab" Exercise)

SPEND TIME ALONE AND TOGETHER WORSHIPPING THE LORD.
BEFORE AND AFTER, RECORD YOUR THOUGHTS AND FEELINGS IN A
JOURNAL. WRITE DOWN CHANGES YOU NOTICE IN YOUR LIFE.

NOTES

_____

_____

_____

_____

_____

_____

_____

_____

_____

_____

_____

_____

_____

_____

_____

_____

_____

_____

_____

_____

_____

Chapter Three

Making Ready the Heart

*"When God measures a man . . .
He puts a tape around the heart
instead of the head."* (Author unknown)

 emember high school days from years gone by?
Maybe even university years? As you thumbed
through the roster of classes, you may have
stumbled on a subject that piqued your interest.
"There it is!" you exclaimed. "That's the course I
really want to take." But all too soon you noticed a tiny asterisk
by the title. Down at the bottom of the page, you discovered
that the asterisk indicated the need for a *prerequisite*—one or
two other courses required first. Chances are good that you
wouldn't have been equipped to absorb the subject matter, even
if you had been able to finagle your way into the course.

In a similar way that schools lay down academic or *head*
prerequisites, God has established some *heart* prerequisites
before we can enjoy worship. First and foremost, only those who
have been brought into a vital relationship with Him through

Jesus Christ are capable of the kind of worship He has in mind. The unbeliever who has yet to be "made new" can't receive spiritual revelation. It sounds like foolishness. Nor can he worship God, no matter how hard he tries. Sin and *self*-consciousness obstruct his view. Jesus reminded the Pharisee, Nicodemus, *"Truly, truly, I say to you, unless one is born again, he cannot see the kingdom of God"* (John 3:3).

In fact, as Chuck Swindoll taught in a message on worship, "The only person *justified* in not worshipping is the unbeliever. For to worship you have to have a Savior, and your Savior has to be the central figure of your life" (emphasis mine).[15]

For those of us who have entered into a Father-child relationship, God gives the divine directive to *love* Him. He said so in the first two of the ten commandments (Exodus 20:1,2). Jesus underscored the same idea in the New Testament, *"You shall love the Lord your God with all your heart, with all your soul, and with all your mind. This is the great and foremost commandment"* (Matthew 22:37,38).

Do these commands imply a passionate expression of our knowledge of God? Are they mandates for a burning dedication of our lives to Him above all else? Yes! To both of these questions—a resounding yes! But we still face a choice. He always gives us the option. Once we've heard Him knocking on the door of our hearts, *we* decide whether or not to open up to Him. Not only at the moment of new birth, but throughout our growing relationship with Him.

> *"Behold, I stand at the door and knock; if anyone hears My voice and opens the door, I will come in to him, and will dine with him, and he with Me."*
>
> Revelation 3:20

By choosing to open up more and more of ourselves to close times with the Lord, we have made the most crucial decision ever. From this point on, every other choice in life presents either an obstacle. . .or an opportunity for that relationship to grow. Major decisions related to a career, a mate, or a home are subject to other people. We actually have only one free choice—whether or not we'll worship the Lord. Sadly enough, most of us never even weigh the options. Other decisions take precedence, and we decide against worship by default.

The Divine Gardener cultivates the heart soil, breaking up the hard lumps of bad attitudes before we can ever begin to worship. God seeks humility in us. A humble heart comes super-naturally when we let go of our own willfulness—and with tremendous results,

> *"Build up, build up, prepare the way, remove every obstacle out of the way of my people." For thus says the high and exalted One who lives forever, whose name is Holy, "I dwell on a high and holy place, and also with the contrite and lowly of spirit in order to revive the spirit of the lowly and to revive the spirit of the contrite."*
>
> Isaiah 57:14b,15

Even Jesus humbled Himself. We have a hard time doing it, but He enables us to take on His thoughts and be broken before the Father,

> *Have this attitude in yourselves which was also in Christ Jesus, who, although He existed in the form of God, did not regard equality with God a thing to be grasped, but emptied Himself, taking the form of a bond-servant, and being made in the likeness of men. And being found in appearance as a man, He humbled Himself by becoming obedient to the point of death, even death on a cross.*
>
> Philippians 2:5-8

Mary of Bethany demonstrated a humble heart that led her into to a beautiful act of worship. We can read her story in John 12. She knelt down in front of a crowd of scoffing onlookers, anointed Jesus' feet with a pound of very expensive perfume, and wiped it away with her long hair. The whole room radiated with the glorious fragrance of her liberal gesture.

Mary's simple expression of love and gratitude to Jesus cost her about a year's earnings! Her heart was so completely "sold out" to the Savior that the cost of her gift didn't matter to her. She wanted no half-measures with which to express her devotion. She gave her best.

Lest we entertain the thought that worshipping is easy. . .or that Christianity consists of singing a few songs on Sunday morning, A.P. Gibbs can set us straight with this comment, "The path of wholehearted discipleship has never been crowded, or popular."[16]

As we embark on the road to becoming genuine worshippers, our actions will undoubtedly be as misunderstood as were Mary's. *But Judas Iscariot, one of His disciples, who was intending to betray Him, said, "Why was this perfume not sold for three hundred denarii, and given to poor people?"* (John 12:4).

Judas reacted with his head instead of his heart. When we get criticized for our enthusiasm, we can take comfort from Jesus' reply to him, *"Let her alone, in order that she may keep it for the day of My burial. For the poor you always have with you, but you do not always have Me"* (John 12:7).

Had Jesus' compassion for the poor run out? No. His whole life demonstrated His love for outcasts and He commands us to help them, too. He was simply setting worship in its rightful place. Mary remained steadfast in her belief in Jesus as the Messiah in the face of the skepticism surrounding her. By her unreserved act of love, she would be the only one to hold the honor of having anointed Jesus for His burial. Can we, like Mary of Bethany, give our sacrificial best to Him?

Jesus Himself agonized and wept for the presence of God. Is it right to think that we can do any less? We must constantly hunger after God's presence, guard against becoming downcast or indifferent, and through it all, remain humble.

As we humble ourselves before God, we will in turn begin to see His greatness more and more. And vice versa. Finally, these two separate acts become one expression of worship. If we can but catch a tiny glimpse of our God as He truly is, our lives will gain eternal perspective. King David expresses both humility and awe in the Psalms,

> *O Lord, our Lord, How majestic is Thy name in all the earth. Who hast displayed Thy splendor above the heavens! When I consider Thy heavens, the work of Thy fingers, the moon and the stars, which Thou has ordained; What is man, that Thou dost take thought of him? And the son of man, that Thou dost care for him?*
>
> Psalm 8:1,3,4

How we do want such worship to be natural for us, too! Only when we're humble can we fully appreciate the majesty of our God. Yet, at the same time, we can never achieve such a heart attitude of humility *until* we see the Lord as He really is. A divine revelation of the magnificence and absolute holiness of God causes healthy brokenness. Rather than causing us to draw back, cringing in fear, these qualities motivate us to worship Him with a passion. It may seem that we have reached an impasse with such apparent contradictions, or antinomies. How can we be humble enough to see God without having seen Him, or to be broken and yet, full of zeal?

What can we do to resolve this dilemma and begin to worship? In our own strength—nothing. Aside from being willing to grow into worshippers and to seek God with our whole hearts, genuine worship lies beyond our grasp. We can only wait upon God to supernaturally reveal Himself as He did with the prophet Isaiah. Notice, again, both humility and awe.

> *. . . I saw the Lord sitting on a throne, lofty and exalted, with the train of His robe filling the temple. Then I said, "Woe is me, for I am ruined! Because I am a*

man of unclean lips; And I live among a people of
unclean lips; For my eyes have seen the King, the Lord
of hosts."

Isaiah 6:1b,5

Isaiah did more than sit on his hands and wait. Our waiting, like his, can be active, not passive. We can rest assured that, as we turn our hearts fully towards God, He *wants* to reveal Himself so we can worship Him. *And you will seek Me and find Me, when you search for Me with all your heart* (Jeremiah 29:13).

Time after time, the Scriptures reveal the Lord of Glory through the eyes of Holy Spirit-inspired servants of old. As we delve into the Word's depths, we can cling to the fact that the same Spirit is waiting to lead *us* to a wealth of truth accessible only through Him. Why not, before continuing, ask the Holy Spirit to open the eyes of our understanding? We, too, want to discover (or rediscover) the glory of the one true God.

FIRE-SEEKER'S COMPANION
Questions for Group Interaction
or Individual Reflection

1. How does enrolling in the "School of the Spirit" compare and contrast to taking academic classes?

2. Does everyone worship? Who can worship *God?* Why?

3. Is being a genuine worshipper easy? Why or why not? How do you feel about that?

4. What is the most important commandment in the Bible? How does it translate to everyday life in the '90's?

5. Does God pressure us to worship? Why or why not? How does our decision to respond to God compare with other major decisions in life?

6. What qualities is God looking for in His worshippers? Does He really want us to "find" Him? Can we stir up in ourselves the ability to worship?

7. Name some biblical examples of genuine worshippers. Why do they qualify for such an esteemed position?

OPEN SHARING: FEEL FREE TO DISCUSS QUESTIONS OR ANYTHING RELATED TO THE CHAPTER THAT MINISTERED TO MEMBERS OF THE GROUP. LET THE HOLY SPIRIT LEAD YOU.

FIRE-STARTER'S PREPARATION
("Lab" Exercise)

SPEND TIME ALONE AND TOGETHER WORSHIPPING THE LORD. BEFORE AND AFTER, RECORD YOUR THOUGHTS AND FEELINGS IN A JOURNAL. WRITE DOWN CHANGES YOU NOTICE IN YOUR LIFE.

NOTES

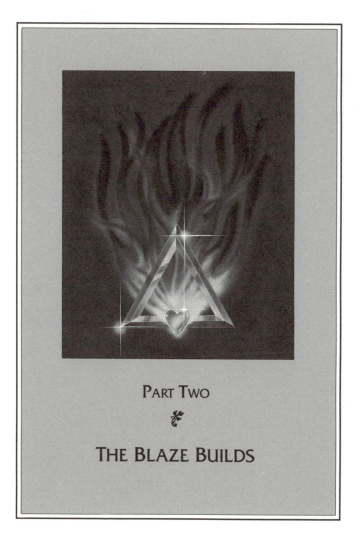

PART TWO

THE BLAZE BUILDS

Chapter Four

Visions of Glory

hink about the first time you took a family trip through beautiful countryside with a view so breathtaking, it roused "oohs" and "ahs" from everyone in the car. Waterfalls. Snowcovered peaks. Rolling hills resplendent with trees in hues of red, orange, yellow and green. Meadows dotted with delicate wild flowers. Waves crashing against a rocky coastline. You probably sat wide-eyed, trying to absorb every trace of beauty.

But supposing that same drive became your only route to work every day—to a job you didn't enjoy. Supposing you faced heavy traffic delays, no-passing curves, on a two-lane road full of potholes. Would the scenery be any less beautiful than the first time? Or would your ability to *see* grow dim?

So it is with our view of God. He is just as magnificent as He has been since eternity. We're the ones who have grown bored. Distracted. Blasé. Or maybe our eyes have *never* really been opened to Him. Let's remove the veil obstructing our glimpse of Him, as if we're wiping off layers of dirt from a master-piece of art forgotten in an attic for years. Someone has said that we don't want for *wonders* around us, only *wonder*. King David never seemed to lose his childlike awe of God.

> *Thine, O Lord, is the greatness and the power and the glory and the victory and the majesty, indeed everything that is in the heavens and the earth; Thine is the dominion, O Lord, and Thou dost exalt Thyself as head over all. Both riches and honor come from Thee, and Thou dost rule over all, and in Thy hand is power and might; and it lies in Thy hand to make great, and to strengthen everyone. Now therefore, our God, we thank Thee, and praise Thy glorious name.*
>
> I Chronicles 29:11-13

David, a "man after God's own heart," expressed true worship so well in those few lines. Through all the trials he had endured in his life, David came to know and appreciate the great God he served. Only from the lips of someone who *loved* God with all his heart, could such freedom of speech flow. Consider these verses, *As the deer pants for the water brooks, so my soul pants for Thee, O God. My soul thirsts for God, for the living God. . .* (Psalm 42:1-2).

We can better understand why David longed so for God when we catch a glimpse of three more visions of His glory which He revealed centuries later to another saint, the Apostle John. May God begin to develop within each one of us David's and John's same heart of love!

The apostle, while in exile on the isle of Patmos, received "pictures" of the Lord in His heavenly realm. John could see Him as he never had before—perhaps because he had no worldly distractions on that island. If we could ask John whether what he saw was worth being banished to such a solitary place, I would venture to say he'd exclaim, *"Oh, yes!"*

Immediately I was in the Spirit: and behold, a throne was standing in heaven, and One sitting on the throne. And He who was sitting was like a jasper stone and a sardius in appearance; and there was rainbow around the throne, like an emerald in appearance...And from the throne proceed flashes of lightning and sounds and peals of thunder. And there were seven lamps of fire burning before the throne, which are the seven Spirits of God.

Revelation 4:2,3,5

No ordinary throne, this one, but the throne of the living God! Exquisite colors, light, powerful sounds and fire envelop Him. In the next passage, God manifests Himself as the eternal Creator. He has existed forever and will continue to exist. He created the universe and its inhabitants for His own pleasure. So God has plenty of company up there. Twenty-four elders and all the heavenly servants surround His throne. What are they doing? Worshipping. God is so awesome, they simply can't help but tell Him.

...and day and night they do not cease to say, Holy, Holy, Holy, is the Lord God, the Almighty, who was and who is and who is to come. And when the living creatures give glory and honor and thanks to Him who sits on the throne, to Him who lives forever and ever, the twenty-four elders will fall down before Him who sits on the throne, and will worship Him who lives forever and ever, and will cast their crowns before the throne, saying, Worthy art Thou, our Lord and our God, to receive glory and honor and power; for Thou didst create all things, and because of Thy will they existed, and were created.

Revelation 4:8-11

He is a holy God who always has, and always will deserve glory and honor. If He's worthy of non-stop adoration from all the hosts of heaven, how much more should we, His children, worship Him here on earth? This scene points toward the first covenant with the children of Israel and to the new covenant with the Gentiles. Many Bible scholars believe that twelve of the twenty-four elders are the patriarchs of the tribes of Israel. The other twelve may be the apostles of Jesus. The union of representatives from the old and new covenants indicates a turning point in God's relationship with man, and yet, His constancy.

As we read John's vision, we might notice that God is seated. He doesn't appear the least bit anxious about the direction things have taken in His creation. For those who fear, because of present circumstances, that God has lost control, this fact provides reassurance. We can draw much comfort in these troubled times. God reigns supreme. Everything proceeds according to His divine foreknowledge.

In the next celestial portrait the hosts of heaven and earth are worshipping God because He meets even the most crucial needs. As the drama first unfolded before John's eyes so long ago, he cried like a baby. No man in, on, or under the earth was found worthy to open and read a very important book— the one with seven seals. An elder comforted him and then showed him more truth about Jesus, the man with whom he had spent three years.

> And one of the elders said to me, "Stop weeping; behold the Lion that is from the tribe of Judah, the Root of David, has overcome so as to open the book and its seven seals." And I saw between the throne (with the four living creatures) and the elders a Lamb standing, as if slain, having seven horns and seven eyes, which are the seven Spirits of God, sent out into the earth. And He came, and He took it out of the right hand of Him who sat on the throne.
>
> Revelation 5:5-7

How did Jesus overcome? Why is He unique in worth, power and position? Because the Father chose Him as His sacrificial Lamb—the only One perfect enough to give His life in exchange for humanity's sin. Jesus deserves our worship. Heaven's citizens certainly broke out singing over that fact.

> *And they sang a new song, saying, "Worthy art Thou to take the book, and to break its seals; for Thou wast slain, and didst purchase for God with Thy blood men from every tribe and tongue and people and nation."*
>
> Revelation 5:9

At the close, John witnessed the most tremendous worship scene of all time. Let's experience the wonder of it right along with him,

> *And I looked, and I heard the voice of many angels around the throne and the living creatures and the elders; and the number of them was myriads of myriads, and thousands of thousands, saying with a loud voice, "Worthy is the Lamb that was slain to receive power and riches and wisdom and might and honor and glory and blessing."*
>
> Revelation 5:11-12

Picture yourself, for a moment, standing among the countless multitudes as they join together to praise the One who gave His life for His creation. How magnificent must be the sound of "thousands of thousands" of voices raised to the glory of God! Could any of us keep quiet on such a wondrous occasion? Our God reigns, and the Lamb with Him!

God's superb plan also revealed to John a vivid contrast—Jesus Christ as the mighty conquering King. This foreshadowed the second coming of the Messiah when He'll no longer be a meek Lamb. He will come as a powerful Ruler to claim His rightful inheritance.

And I saw heaven opened; and behold, a white horse, and He who sat upon it is called Faithful and True; and in righteousness He judges and wages war. And His eyes are a flame of fire, and upon His head are many diadems; and He has a name written upon Him which no one knows except Himself. And He is clothed with a robe dipped in blood; and His name is called The Word of God. And the armies which are in heaven, clothed in fine linen, white and clean, were following Him on white horses. And from His mouth comes a sharp sword, so that with it He may smite the nations; and He will rule them with a rod of iron and He treads the wine press of the fierce wrath of God, the Almighty. And on His robe and on His thigh He has a name written, "King of Kings, and Lord of Lords."

Revelation 19:11-16

Hallelujah! We can't mistake this message: Jesus stands alone as King above all kings and Lord above all lords. He's set apart. Absolutely unique. When He returns with His army He will enforce total victory. We have this assurance from God Himself. The devil's time of torment will come to an end; indeed, by faith, has come to an end already.

Isn't it plain why John saw God seated on the throne and not nervously "wringing His hands?" Jesus will exact judgment upon those who reject the free gift He offers. As the living Word, He will judge the world by the Word. Satan, the fallen angels and those he has deceived will burn in the lake of fire forever—which leads us to one more reason to worship God. We have been inducted into the heavenly army to serve as priests and kings, and we'll escape this everlasting death.

Yes, as the song goes, there *is* victory in Jesus! What the Father began with creation, prophesied in the Old Testament and fulfilled in the New Testament, He will bring to a close when the King returns. His ways are higher than our ways, and His thoughts higher than our thoughts (Isaiah 55:9). We will not always understand what we see happening around us. But if we keep our eyes on the Lord, we will be able to say, "He's faithful. I *know* He is." God gives us the promise in Romans 8:28 that eventually all things work into an overall plan for good. For a season, it seems to be a lie. But how secure are His promises? Can we really depend on His Word? He says we can.

> *For as the rain and the snow come down from heaven, and do not return without watering the earth, and making it bear and sprout, and furnishing seed to the sower and bread to the eater; so shall My word be which goes forth from My mouth; It shall not return to Me empty, without accomplishing what I desire, and without succeeding in the matter for which I sent it.*
>
> Isaiah 55:10,11

Will we join with King David and John? How can we do anything less than offer high praises to our God for such powerful promises. Let's proclaim the glory of the Lord they loved. And we'll find more reasons to worship after we learn more about Him in the next chapter.

FIRE-SEEKER'S COMPANION
Questions for Group Interaction
or Individual Reflection

1. Has God become less awe-inspiring today than in biblical days? What causes a "ho-hum" attitude toward Him in your life?

2. Briefly, what did God show John? Where was John at the time and why do you suppose God showed him all that He did?

3. Describe the Father. What position is He in and what does that reveal about Him? How about the others present in the scene? Who are they and what are they doing?

4. Why did John cry? Who and what comforted him? What is all the celebration about?

5. Compare and contrast the two glimpses John had of Jesus.

6. How can we be assured of God's dependability? What picture from nature does He use to remind us of this?

7. Can John's visions of God help you to worship Him better today? Why?

OPEN SHARING: FEEL FREE TO DISCUSS QUESTIONS OR ANYTHING RELATED TO THE CHAPTER THAT MINISTERED TO MEMBERS OF THE GROUP. LET THE HOLY SPIRIT LEAD YOU.

Fire-starter's Preparation
("Lab" Exercise)

SPEND TIME ALONE AND TOGETHER WORSHIPPING THE LORD. BEFORE AND AFTER, RECORD YOUR THOUGHTS AND FEELINGS IN A JOURNAL. WRITE DOWN CHANGES YOU NOTICE IN YOUR LIFE.

NOTES

Chapter Five

Getting to Know Him

n choosing a life partner for marriage, wise singles want to be sure they know the person very well. Minimal guesswork. A bride-to-be's checklist might read something like this: *"How does he treat me and the people I care about?" "Does he love children?" "What are his values and goals?" "What kind of character does he show under stress?" "What has he ac-complished in life up until now?"* The more good traits, the better. The flower of love blooms in the light of desirable qualities. Until those spouses get a closer look—after marriage. Then they notice numerous flaws. Their partner leaves the cap off the toothpaste, throws dirty clothes in a heap on the floor, and spends too much money. Love can wither on the vine in a hurry.

But the more we know about God, the better He looks. We'll never discover any bad habits or shady traits about Him, no matter how deep we dig. We'll just find more evidences of His unique worth. Of His perfection. . . and our imperfections that need Him to fill in the gaps.

In *Visions of Glory* we focused on the sublime, celestial side of God. We will see Him like that in heaven, but we can also know Him in a practical way now. Have you ever asked yourself the question, "Who is God, really?" What comes to mind when someone speaks of Jesus Christ? A random group of people asked these questions would no doubt give many descriptions, some of a sound scriptural basis and some, otherwise.

A. W. Tozer has said that our most important thought is our conception of God. It should be as close as possible to the truth. Only then can we "worship Him in Spirit and in truth." It's critical that we grasp as much as we can about the One who created us, loves us and died for us, and waits for the fulfillment of all things. John gave us a peek at the future, so let's gaze back at the past—which, of course, is all the same to God.

We can uncover a wealth of insight into the nature of God by looking at His different names. In the Hebrew language a name held much more significance than in English today. It expressed the nature, character, or purpose of that which it named. To pursue our understanding of who God is, we can best begin with how He revealed Himself to the children of Israel.

Elohim

In the first verse of the first chapter of the first book of the Bible, we've all read or heard, *God created. . .* The word for God here is *Elohim*, and in it reside the first clues to God's identity. Elohim, a plural word, indicates His triune nature and His supremacy as the Creator. The One we worship is the *eternal, immortal, invisible, the only wise God* (I Timothy 1:17). He is the Father, Son and Holy Spirit, as well as *our* Father, *our* Lord, and the Spirit living in every believer.

The worship of the eternal God through His eternal Spirit is far more than merely touching eternity; it is actually entering into an activity that is eternal in every dimension... Worshippers reach from before the world until after the world and join the angels of heaven in worship and adoration of God, *"the Alpha and the Omega, the Beginning and the End...who is and who was and who is to come, the Almighty."*[17]

In a memorable message on worship at a Fellowship of Christian Athletes meeting, Anne Graham Lotz described God as being "Eternity, Divinity and Activity." That sums up Elohim very well. God is eternal, and therefore, not bound by the restrictions of time. He exists outside of time itself. As the Apostle Peter noted, a thousand years may be as one day in His sight. Space cannot bind Him, either. In His omnipresence and omniscience, He is present always and everywhere. He sees and knows all things.

On only one occasion has God limited Himself to the boundaries of time, and He did that for us! He chose to become a man. He decided to become part of His creation in order to rescue it. When Jesus came in the flesh, He lived under the same rules He expected man to obey. Then the Lord went one step further. He submitted Himself to His own invention and allowed it to crucify Him.

God expressed His divinity through creation, but He is much greater than anything in it. He is set apart. Elohim created all and controls all, yet, remains as separate from His creation as an artist from his painting. A painting on canvas is but a reflection of the artist, not the artist himself. So does the universe only reflect Elohim.

When we speak of the activity of God, we refer to the Creator as we see Him in the opening chapters of Genesis and the first chapter of John. Our Lord Jesus (the Word) certainly demonstrated an active part of the Trinity,

❦

In the beginning was the Word, and the Word was with God, and the Word was God. He was in the beginning with God. All things came into being by Him, and apart from Him nothing came into being that has come into being.

John 1:1-3

Let's worship Him, the eternal Creator, Elohim!

El Shaddai

This name appears in Genesis 17:1 as God's declaration to Abram. He said, *"I am El Shaddai: Almighty God."* God's name combined His great and glorious nature (El) with His ability to provide (Shaddai). The meaning of Shaddai comes close to "a mother's breast." In the same way that a mother's breast nourishes, comforts, and satisfies a helpless baby, so does our God do for us. In comparison to the vast universe, we *are* helpless.

We might note that only after God declared Himself as El Shaddai, did He establish the covenant with Abram and change his name to Abraham. God was stating His intent and ability to fulfill His part in the relationship with Abraham and all of his descendants. Up until that time, people knew God as the Creator in an impersonal sort of way, but with this covenant, things changed. God unveiled a new revelation of His nature and a unique relationship began.

Let's worship Him, Almighty God, El Shaddai!

Jehovah-Jireh

The meaning of this name occurs in the passage where God commanded Abraham to offer his precious, long-awaited son as a sacrifice. The Lord required such obedience from Abraham as a means of testing or proving his faithfulness. Abraham needed to learn to trust God implicitly. Would God provide a means for his son Isaac to return with him from the mountain? Abraham believed so. His words to his servants even before climbing the mount of sacrifice showed his faith,

> *On the third day Abraham raised his eyes and saw the place from a distance. And Abraham said unto his young men, "Stay here with the donkey, and I and the lad will go yonder; and* **we will worship and return to you.**"
>
> Genesis 22:4

Abraham's confidence in El Shaddai never wavered. He may not have known the details of how Isaac would survive, but he knew that God would be faithful to His earlier promises. As we read further on, God demonstrated His undisputed authority. All He required? Abraham's unquestioning obedience,

> *And Abraham stretched out his hand, and took the knife to slay his son. But the angel of the Lord called to him from heaven, and said, "Abraham, Abraham!" And he said, "Here I am." And He said, "Do not stretch out your hand against the lad, and do nothing to him; for now I know that you fear God, since you have not withheld your son, your only son, from Me." Then Abraham raised his eyes and looked, and behold, behind him a ram caught in the thicket by his horns; and Abraham went and took the ram, and offered him up for a burnt offering in the place of his son. And Abraham called the name of that place (Jehovah-jireh), the Lord will provide, as it is said to this day, "In the mount of the Lord it will be provided."*
>
> Genesis 22:10-14

Abraham's tremendous act of faith foreshadowed the day when another Father would offer His only Son. Only He wouldn't spare His life—on purpose. Let's worship Him, the Lord our provider, Jehovah-jireh!

Jehovah-Nissi

This name means, "the Lord our banner," the One high above us and around whom we rally in difficult times. He goes ahead of us in battle (spiritual or natural) so we know which direction to travel. When we look up at Him, He boosts our confidence and bolsters our courage so we can keep fighting to the end.

After their miraculous deliverance from Egypt, the children of Israel confronted the Amalekite tribe. In this first battle, God revealed Himself as Jehovah-nissi through Moses,

> So Moses said to Joshua, "Choose men for us, and go out, fight against Amalek. Tomorrow I will station myself on the top of the hill with the staff of God in my hand." And Joshua did as Moses told him, and fought against Amalek; and Moses, Aaron, and Hur went up to the top of the hill. So it came about when Moses held his hand up that Israel prevailed, and when he let his hand down, Amalek prevailed. But Moses' hands were heavy. Then they took a stone and put it under him, and he sat on it; and Aaron and Hur supported his hands, one on one side and one on the other. Thus his hands were steady until the sun set. So Joshua overwhelmed Amalek and his people with the edge of the sword. Then the Lord said to Moses, "Write this in a book as a memorial, and recite it to Joshua, that I will utterly blot out the memory of Amalek from under heaven." And Moses built an altar, and named it (Jehovah-nissi) the Lord is my banner.

> Exodus 17:9-15

Each time Moses held up the rod of God the people gained enough strength to overcome the enemy. When the rod came down they lost ground. This rod, then, provided a visible standard or ensign around which the people rallied, and when it remained high in the air, God performed feats of victory. Symbolic of God Himself, the rod pointed forward through the ages to Jesus. Like Moses, who built an altar to commemorate the Lord's name and His role in battle, we might remind ourselves often of the One high above us. We gather around Jehovah-nissi, and exalt Him who *always causes us to triumph* (II Corinthians 2:14).

Let's worship Him, the Lord our banner, Jehovah-nissi!

Jehovah-Rophe

After the children of Israel crossed the Red Sea by a mighty miracle, they languished in the wilderness without water for three days. When they finally found water it was too bitter to drink. What disappointment! Once again, God proved He was truly their provider. Through the miraculous, He confirmed this new revelation of His nature as their healer, Jehovah-rophe,

> *So the people grumbled at Moses, saying, "What shall we drink?" Then he cried out to the Lord, and the Lord showed him a tree; and he threw it into the waters, and the waters became sweet. There He made for them a statute and regulation, and there He tested them. And He said, "If you will give earnest heed to the voice of the Lord your God, and do what is right in His sight, and give ear to His commandments, and keep all His statutes, I will put none of the diseases on you which I have put on the Egyptians; for I, the Lord, am (Jehovah-rophe) your healer."*

Exodus 15:24-26

Let's worship Him, the Lord our healer, Jehovah-rophe!

Jehovah-Shalom

This name means "the Lord our peace." We could use a calming hand upon us during these troubled times. Gideon met God as Jehovah-shalom at a crucial point in his life and in history. The people of Israel were enduring extreme hardship under the oppressive power of the Midianites. They cried out for deliverance. God responded to their plea by sending an angel to tell Gideon he had been chosen to be the instrument of their release.

Skepticism and fear gripped Gideon's heart. He didn't feel up to the dangerous task and reminded the Lord why. He came from the poorest, weakest clan, and he was the least among *them,* no less. That didn't bother God. He told Gideon He would be with him. Gideon offered a present to the Lord of bread and meat and said he needed a more dramatic assurance of God's favor. He got it. With a touch of the angel's staff to the rock, fire sprang up and consumed Gideon's offering. But then he felt more afraid than ever.

> *When Gideon saw that he was an angel of the Lord, he said, "Alas, O Lord God! For now I have seen the angel of the Lord face to face." And the Lord said to him, "Peace to you, do not fear; you shall not die." Then Gideon built an altar there to the Lord and named it (Jehovah-shalom) the Lord is peace.*
>
> Judges 6:22-24

This revelation came at a time of national unrest and in the face of insurmountable odds. The same holds true for us today. No matter what circumstances we face. . . despite how things look, or how we feel in the midst of turmoil. . .we have a wonderful assurance. Our peace does not depend upon anyone or anything. *God* is our peace.

Let's worship Him, the Lord our peace, Jehovah-shalom!

Jehovah-Tsidkenu

All our own righteous deeds are as *filthy rags* before a holy God, the Word reminds us in Isaiah 64:6. We need something outside ourselves to make us clean. God gave us this name, "the Lord our righteousness," in a prophetic word to Jeremiah.

> *"Behold, the days are coming," declares the Lord, "when I will raise up for David a righteous Branch, and he will reign as king and act wisely, and do justice and righteousness in the land. In His days Judah will be saved, and Israel will dwell securely: and this is His name by which he will be called, (Jehovah-tsidkenu) The Lord our righteousness."*
>
> Jeremiah 23:5,6

Jehovah-tsidkenu points forward to the coming of Jesus as the perfect Lamb of God. We find in the writing of the Apostle Paul that Jesus, who knew no sin, took on the burden of sin so that we might become the righteousness of God in Him (II Corinthians 5:21). In a kind of divine exchange, we give Him our sin; He gives us His holiness. We turn in our old, dirty clothes; He dresses us in a brand new set of white garments.

Let's worship Him, the Lord our righteousness, Jehovah-tsidkenu!

Jehovah-M'kaddesh

Here we find another facet of God's nature, later manifested in the Son of God—Jehovah-m'kaddesh, the Lord our sanctifier. In addition to washing us clean inwardly (righteousness), He sets us apart as a unique, holy people of His own. His purposes become ours, and He uses us as He sees fit. In the Old Testament, keeping one day of the week as a special "Lord's day" provided an outward demonstration of His people's uniqueness. God gave the commandment to Moses,

> *"But as for you, speak to the sons of Israel, saying,*
> *'You shall surely observe My sabbaths; for this is a*
> *sign between Me and you throughout your genera-*
> *tions, that you may know that I am (Jehovah-m'kad-*
> *desh) the Lord who sanctifies you.'"*
>
> Exodus 31:13

How important that we realize our God sanctifies us, not we ourselves, *Therefore Jesus also, that He might sanctify the people through His own blood...* (Hebrews 13:12). *And such were some of you; but you were washed, but you were sanc-tified, but you were justified in the name of the Lord Jesus Christ, and in the Spirit of our God* (I Corinthians 6:11). We have only to accept what Jesus already accomplished on the cross. Then our habits *outside* will demonstrate to others what He has done for us *inside*.

Let's worship Him, the Lord our sanctifier, who distinguishes us from all others, Jehovah-m'kaddesh!

Jehovah-Shammah

God revealed Himself to Ezekiel as Jehovah-shammah, the One who is always present. The prophet had a vision of the Holy City the Lord will establish upon the new earth at the close of the age. New Jerusalem will be God's dwelling place forever, *The city shall be 18,000 cubits round about; and the name of the city from that day shall be, (Jehovah-shammah), the Lord is there.*

This passage does speak of a future event, but applies to us today, as well. God still meets with man in His tabernacle, or temple. We, the members of His Body, are living temples in which His Holy Spirit dwells (I Corinthians 3:16). Jesus promised in Matthew 28:20, . . .*lo, I am with you always, even to the end of the age.* On that glorious day we will walk the streets of New Jerusalem and see God face to face.

Let's worship Him, the Lord who is ever present with us, Jehovah-shammah!

❧

Jehovah-Rohi

Almost everyone knows that beautiful psalm of King David: *The Lord is my shepherd; I shall not want...*(Psalm 23:1). Jesus reminds us of the identity of the tender-hearted shepherd and how we can recognize Him,

> *"I am the good shepherd: the good shepherd lays down his life for the sheep. He who is a hireling, and not a shepherd, who is not the owner of the sheep, beholds the wolf coming, and leaves the sheep, and flees, and the wolf snatches them, and scatters them."*
>
> John 10:11,12

Without a leader to follow, we wander astray as easily as simple-minded sheep. They don't even know when they're lost. Our watchful, gentle shepherd leads us to quiet waters of His Holy Spirit where we quench our thirst and to rich pastures of His Word where He guards us as we eat our fill. In that beautiful spot, He binds up our wounds and pursues us if we should wander off. He heals our broken hearts and leads us down paths of blessing because His name is at stake. When He makes a promise, He keeps it.

Let's worship Him, our good shepherd, Jehovah-rohi!

Jehovah-Elyon

This name elevates God as the Lord Most High. There is none higher than He! *For the Lord Most High is to be feared, a great King over all the earth* (Psalm 47:2). *For Thou art the Lord Most High over all the earth; Thou art exalted far above all gods* (Psalm 97:9).

Let's worship Him, the Lord Most High, Jehovah-elyon!

Jehovah-Hoseenu

Jehovah-hoseenu is the Lord our Maker, our personal Creator with whom we have a covenant relationship. This name acknowledges God as more than just the Creator of nature and other living things. He has a right to us, as well—our time, talent, treasure and thoughts. *Come, let us worship and bow down; Let us kneel before the Lord our Maker* (Psalm 95:6).

Let's worship Him, the Lord our Maker, Jehovah-hoseenu!

Jehovah-Eloheenu

In this name God declares Himself as the Lord our God. He is both Lord and a holy, set-apart God only to those of us who have entered into a covenant with Him.

Exalt the Lord our God, and worship at His footstool; Holy is He. . .O Lord our God, Thou didst answer them; Thou wast a forgiving God to them, and yet an avenger of their evil deeds. Exalt the Lord our God, and worship at His holy hill, for holy is the Lord our God.

Psalm 99:5,8,9

Let's worship Him, the Lord our God, Jehovah-eloheenu!

Jehovah-Elohim

We find the first of many occurrences of this title, the Lord God, in the second chapter of Genesis, *These are the generations of the heavens and of the earth when they were created, in the day that the Lord God made the earth and the heaven* (Genesis 2:4). This name, like others, proclaims the Self-Existent One, the Eternal Creator of all things, in covenant relationship with His people.

Let's worship Him, the Lord God, Jehovah-elohim!

Jehovah-Eloheka

When God gave Moses the ten commandments, He said He was Jehovah-eloheka, Israel's Lord,

"I am the Lord your God, who brought you out of the land of Egypt, out of the house of slavery. . . You shall not worship them or serve them; for I, the Lord your God, am a jealous God. . . You shall not take the name of the Lord your God in vain . . ."

Exodus 20:2,5,7

Worship Him, spiritual Israel—the Lord your God, Jehovah-eloheka!

Jehovah-Elohay

God reveals Himself in even more of a personal relationship with His people. Each individual who knows Him can call Him, "The Lord *my* God," the One who cares about me, no matter what events take place in the world. The prophet, Zechariah, referred to Him as such,

. . . Then the Lord, my God, will come, and all the holy ones with Him! And it will come about in that day that there will be no light; the luminaries will dwindle. For it will be a unique day which is known to the Lord, neither day nor night, but it will come about that at evening time there will be light. And the Lord will be king over all the earth; in that day the Lord will be the only one, and His name the only one.

Zechariah 14:5-7,9

Let each of us worship Him, the Lord my God, Jehovah-elohay!

Jehovah-Sabaoth

Perhaps the most famous passage in the Old Testament recounts the story of David and Goliath. It contains further revelation of God's character as Jehovah-sabaoth, the Lord of heaven's entire army of spiritual beings. You remember the scenario. An arrogant Philistine giant, Goliath, had been taunting the Israelite army over and over, until finally a champion emerged—the young shepherd boy. But this unlikely warrior candidate knew his God. He had depended on Him when he faced wild animals who threatened his sheep. David ventured forth, not with the cumbersome, unfamiliar weapons of Saul's army, but with his faithful staff and sling. Watch the thrilling encounter,

> *And the Philistine said to David, "Am I a dog, that you come to me with sticks?" And the Philistine cursed David by his gods. And the Philistine also said to David, "Come to me, and I will give your flesh to the birds of the sky and the beasts of the field." Then David said to the Philistine, "You come to me with a sword, a spear, and a javelin, but I come to you **in the name of the Lord of Hosts** (Jehovah-sabaoth), the God of the armies of Israel, whom you have taunted."*
>
> I Samuel 17:43-45

David charged and defeated Israel's intimidating enemy because he knew the name of His power source. He advanced in the strength of the God he served. We, too, can defeat every "giant" in the powerful name of the Lord—by His authority.

Let's worship Him, the Lord of hosts, Jehovah-sabaoth!

Oh yes, let's worship the One who can meet every single need. God gave the Jehovah covenant names to the children of Israel, beginning with Abraham. Gentile nations had accepted the idea of an Eternal Creator, but did not know Him as their Lord and Master.

❦

When He declared He was Jehovah (Lord) to Abraham, He formed a special union with mankind. No longer could His own people mistake Him for a distant Creator watching His creation from "afar." From that moment on He became Lord, Master and King who would forever be personally involved with His subjects.

In that position, He promised to protect, to guide and direct, to provide for, and to love His people as a father loves his children. This relationship did not apply to all the inhabitants of the earth, but only to Abraham and his descendants who came to Him by faith. God required one thing in return: love and obedience.

It may appear that the promises to the children of Israel have no relevance for the Christian today. "Weren't the covenant names for Abraham and his descendants?" you might wonder. Yes, but these promises still apply to us, too. We will see how this is possible, even though most of us cannot call Abraham our ancestor.

Faith, the Word tells us, motivated Abraham to do all he did. Faith in Jesus Christ enables humans to be born again. Ephesians 2:8,9 tells us, *For by grace you have been saved through faith; and that not of yourselves, it is the gift of God.* God becomes our Father, too, because of all that Jesus Christ accomplished through His life, death and resurrection. By faith in what Jesus did, we become recipients of a heritage given only to the Jewish nation. What a fantastic truth! The Apostle Paul explains this phenomenon further in his letter to the Galatians,

> *And the Scripture, foreseeing that God would justify the Gentiles by faith, preached the gospel beforehand to Abraham, saying, "All the nations shall be blessed in you." So then those who are of faith are blessed with Abraham, the believer. Christ redeemed us from the curse of the Law, having become a curse for us; for it is written, "Cursed is everyone who hangs on a tree"—in order that in Christ Jesus the blessing of*

Abraham might come to the Gentiles, so that we might receive the promise of the Spirit through faith. For you are all sons of God through faith in Jesus Christ. And if you belong to Christ, then you are Abraham's offspring, heirs according to promise.

Galatians 3:8-9,13-14,26-29

To summarize then, who do we worship?

He is, first of all, Elohim, the Eternal Creator who always was and always will be, and He is El Shaddai, our strength, the source of comfort, confidence and nourishment. He is Jehovah-jireh, who has seen our needs and provided for them even before we know them, and Jehovah-nissi, the One who still calls us to rally around Him so He can perform miracles on our behalf. He is Jehovah-rophe, our kind Physician and Jehovah-shalom, our peace in every situation, regardless of how circumstances may appear. Jehovah-tsidkenu gives us His righteousness in exchange for our sins and Jehovah-m'kaddesh sets us apart for His purposes through His own precious blood. He is Jehovah-shammah who is always present with us and in us, and Jehovah-rohi, the gentle Shepherd who leads us to quiet waters and green pastures.

Jehovah-elyon is the Most High exalted above all and Jehovah-hoseenu knows us even in our mother's womb. Jehovah-eloheenu is the Lord our God; Jehovah-eloheka is the Lord, Israel's God, and Jehovah-elohay is the Lord my God. Finally, He is Jehovah-sabaoth, the Lord of all the hosts of heaven and earth.

Even though God has many different facets and a name for each of His characteristics, He remains a trinity—Father, Son and Holy Spirit. Here in the concept of the Trinity we find an antinomy. This, as we learned in an earlier chapter, consists of two ideas that appear contradictory, but are both true. In the divine Trinity, there are three who are God, and yet, *the Lord our God is one* (Deuteronomy 6:4).

All true believers worship God the Father, the first Person of the Trinity, because He desires worship. *But an hour is coming, and now is, when the true worshippers shall worship the Father in spirit and truth; for such people the Father seeks to be His worshippers* (John 4:23).

We worship our Father because He is the holy Father and the righteous Father (John 17:16,35). He is the Father of glory (Ephesians 1:17), and the Father of light, from whom all good things come (James 1:17). He is the Father of mercies (II Corinthians 1:3), and the Father of our Lord Jesus Christ (Ephesians 1:3, I Peter 1:3 and Timothy 3:16). Not only do we worship Him for who He is, but for what He has done. Above all, the Father loves us very much.

> *For God so loved the world, that He gave His only begotten Son, that whosoever believes in Him should not perish, but have eternal life.*
>
> John 3:16

> *The Lord appeared to him from afar, saying, "I have loved you with an everlasting love; therefore I have drawn you with lovingkindness."*
>
> Jeremiah 31:3

He showed the depth of His love when He sent His own Son for us (I John 1:9) that we might be sons of God (I John 3:1). By the Father of our Lord we have been blessed with all spiritual blessings, chosen, predestined for adoption, made acceptable, redeemed and forgiven, and made aware of the mystery of His will (Ephesians 1:3-9). Finally, the Father has made it possible through His gift for us to enter into His presence to worship Him,

> *Since therefore, brethren, we have confidence to enter the holy place by the blood of Jesus, by a new and living way which He inaugurated for us through the*

*veil, that is, His flesh, and since we have a great priest
over the house of God, let us draw near with a sincere
heart in full assurance of faith, having our hearts
sprinkled clean from an evil conscience and our
bodies washed with pure water.*

Hebrews 10:19-22

Yes, the Father has prepared the way for us to worship Him
through the Son, our Lord and Savior. Even the Son Himself
proclaimed, *"I am the way, the truth and the life: no man cometh
unto the Father but by me"* (John 14:6).

Calling God "Father" is a tremendous privilege. Did you
know that one particular major world religion has almost one
hundred names for their god, but "Father" doesn't show up
once? That's because no path exists other than Jesus, the Word.
We worship Jesus Christ, like the Father, for who He is, for what
He has done, what He is doing and for what He is yet to do.

Jesus, the Living Word, played a premier role in the
creation of the universe.

*In the beginning was the Word, and the Word was with
God, and the Word was God. He was in the beginning
with God. All things came into being by Him, and
apart from Him nothing came into being that came
into being. And the Word became flesh, and dwelt
among us, and we beheld His glory, glory as of the
only begotten from the Father, full of grace and truth.*

John 1:1-3,14

*For by Him all things were created, both in the
heavens and on earth, visible and invisible, whether
thrones or dominions or rulers or authorities—all
things have been created by Him and for Him.*

Colossians 1:16

We find also that Jesus revealed the Father to the world.

How? By taking on flesh and blood to walk among us. *No man has seen God at any time; the only begotten Son, who is in the bosom of the Father, He has explained Him* (John 1:18). *"He who has seen me has seen the Father. . ."* (John 14:9b). A child once said that Jesus came as "God with skin on." He became the fulfillment of the characteristics God communicated through His covenant names. In Jesus' own words,

> *"And now, glorify Thou Me together with Thyself, Father, with the glory which I had with Thee before the world was. **I manifested Thy name** to the men who Thou gavest Me out of the world; Thine they were, and Thou gavest them to Me, and they have kept Thy word."*
>
> John 17:5,6

In the Old Testament, when Moses asked God His name, He replied, *"I AM WHO I AM"* (Exodus 3:14). Throughout the gospel of John, Jesus announced who He was in what some scholars have called the "I AM revelations." How similar in nature they are to the covenant names just studied! No coincidence, of course.

> *"**I am the bread of life**; he who comes to Me shall not hunger, and he who believes in Me shall never thirst."*
>
> John 6:35

> *"**I am the light of the world**; he who follows Me shall not walk in the darkness, but shall have the light of life."*
>
> John 8:12

> *"**I am the door**; if anyone enters through Me, he shall be saved, and shall go in and out and find pasture."*
>
> John 10:9

*"I am the good shepherd; the good shepherd lays
down his life for the sheep. . .I am the good shepherd,
and I know my own, and My own know Me."*

John 10:11,14

*"I am the resurrection and the life; he who believes
in Me shall live even if he dies."*

John 11:25

*"I am the way, the truth, and the life; no one comes
to the Father but through Me."*

John 14:6

*"I am the true vine, and My Father is the vinedresser.
Every branch in Me that does not bear fruit, He takes
away; and every branch that bears fruit, He prunes
it, that it may bear more fruit."*

John 15:1,2

To all those who belong to Him, Jesus embodies every
promise inherent in the Old Testament name Jehovah. Jesus
not only provided food from heaven the way the Father sent
manna in the wilderness; He *is* the Bread of life that came down
from above. He is the true Vine who always bears healthy fruit
and the good Shepherd who gave His life for the sheep.

We will never walk in darkness because He is the Light that
disperses darkness. Jesus is the only way to the Father; in fact,
He's the very door through which we enter. He died, but that
marked a new beginning. He gives us true life because He rose
from the dead and lives forevermore. He doesn't *have* life. . .He
is life itself! Jesus, the man, was God incarnate. The prophet,
Isaiah, foretold this centuries earlier,

*For a child will be born to us, a son will be given to
us; and the government will rest on His shoulders;*

*and His name will be called Wonderful Counselor,
Mighty God, Eternal Father, Prince of Peace.*

Isaiah 9:6

As the Prince of Peace, He lived a holy life in perfect obedience to His heavenly Father, and finished the work He was
given. After His resurrection Jesus ascended into heaven, where
He now sits at the right hand of the Father. There He presides
as Head over the Church. At the end of the age, He will return
to fulfill His promise to His people,

*For the Lord Himself will descend from heaven with
a shout, with the voice of the archangel, and with the
trumpet of God; and the dead in Christ shall rise first.
Then we who are alive and remain shall be caught
up together with them in the clouds to meet the Lord
in the air, and thus we shall always be with the Lord.*

I Thessalonians 4:16,17

Hallelujah! How can we keep from responding in worship
and adoration? Our future will make present suffering worth
it. We serve such a glorious God!

These passages have given us more insight into the nature
of the Father and the Son. What about the Holy Spirit, the third
Person of the Trinity? In the Old Testament the word, "ruach,"
was translated into spirit two hundred thirty times. In the New
Testament, the word, "pneuma" has a similar meaning. Both
words imply an invisible force, akin to the breath of God. Yet
He's a person. Through the Holy Spirit, God communicates with
us today.

Should we worship the Holy Spirit? The Word doesn't
encourage us to worship Him, although He is just as much God.
The Spirit Himself *leads, instructs,* and *empowers* us to worship.
He guides us, through the Word of God, to an ever-increasing
appreciation of the Father and Son. A balanced diet of

Scriptures and the Spirit makes the healthiest Christians. By the way, the Holy Spirit will never persuade a believer to do anything contrary to the Word of God. He will lead the believer to a deeper and fuller revelation of the Divine.

Most Christians have read parts of the Bible. Yet, they admit they can't understand much of it—especially the more profound divine truth. Only the Holy Spirit can reveal the shades of meaning. Relying totally on His guidance, we submit our entire beings—spirits, souls and bodies—to Him. That may take awhile because we cherish our independence. We surrender little by little. When we do though, our study and prayer times, as well as our praise and worship, will produce much spiritual fruit.

As mere human beings, we simply don't know how to worship God. I told you how hard it's been for me. We, like the Israelites who danced around the golden calf, prefer to enjoy something we can *see* and *touch*. Yes, I know the Holy Spirit lives within every Christian, but only gradually do we learn to follow Him. Then we can *worship in Spirit and in truth.*

Many evangelical services and much "gospel" music cater only to man's emotions which stem from the soul (intellect, will and emotions) and not the spirit. In order for us to truly worship, or for that matter, to experience a genuine "new birth" and lasting transformation, our spirits must join with God's Spirit. Bob Mumford said it concisely, "When Spirit and spirit meet—there is worship!"[18]

God is love, Scripture informs us. Throughout the Bible we see the Holy Spirit exhibiting the three characteristics that make up the love triangle. Not only do these elements comprise our love for Him, but they reflect His loving nature. *He is* the ultimate in *knowledge, covenant* and *worship.* The same principle applies to the Father and Son, of course, because they are one God. For our purposes here though, we'll look at the verses referring to the Holy Spirit.

He has knowledge and intelligence. We learn that He knows, speaks, intercedes, teaches, hears and guides,

And in the same way the Spirit also helps our weakness; for we do not know how to pray as we should, but the Spirit Himself intercedes for us with groanings too deep for words. . .

Romans 8:26-27

"But the Helper, the Holy Spirit, whom the Father will send in My name, He will teach you all things, and bring to your remembrance all that I have said to you."

John 14:26

"But when He, the Spirit of truth comes, He will guide you into all the truth; for He will not speak on His own initiative, but whatever He hears, He will speak; and He will disclose to you what is to come."

John 16:13

Does the Holy Spirit have a will and exhibit a covenant kind of commitment toward us? Yes, for He struggles to bring our will under submission and chastens us, *Then the Lord said, "My Spirit shall not strive with man forever, because he also is flesh. . ."* (Genesis 6:3).

For the flesh sets its desire against the Spirit, and the Spirit against the flesh; for these are in opposition to one another, so that you may not do the things that you please.

Galatians 5:17

The Holy Spirit is motivated by strong passions, also, because we know He was grieved, and can be stifled or despised, *And do not grieve the Holy Spirit of God, by whom you were sealed for the day of redemption* (Ephesians 4:30). *Do not quench the Spirit (I Thessalonians 5:19).*

*How much severer punishment do you think he will
deserve who has trampled under foot the Son of God,
and has regarded as unclean the blood of the covenant by which he was sanctified, and has insulted the
Spirit of grace?*

Hebrews 10:29

The Holy Spirit has many titles in the Word of God, as well
as many different abilities and functions. Above all, He is
absolutely holy. He is the Spirit of truth and our Comforter. He
is the Spirit of God, the Spirit of grace, the Spirit of Christ, the
Spirit of glory, and the Spirit of promise.

During creation the Holy Spirit brooded over the waters
of the chaotic earth. He inspired all Scripture (II Timothy 3:16);
was present in Christ's incarnation (Luke 1:25); in Jesus' life
on earth (Matthew 3:16) and in His death. Through the power
of the eternal Spirit, He offered Himself to the Father (Hebrews
9:14). In Jesus' post-resurrection ministry, *He, through the Holy
Ghost, had given commandments unto the apostles* (Acts 1:2).
Everywhere, we observe the Holy Spirit at work!

In the world, the Holy Spirit convicts man of sin and of his
need for a Savior. Man recognizes his unrighteousness and his
inability to meet God's requirements for holiness. Those who
do accept Jesus' sacrifice as a gift are sealed with the Spirit
until the day of redemption. This seal acts as a kind of
"downpayment" and assures us that God will fulfill all His
promises. (Some information on the Trinity is from **Worship,**
by A.P. Gibbs[19])

How does He know our every need? *For the eyes of the
Lord move to and fro throughout the earth that He may strongly
support those whose heart is completely His* (II Chronicles 16:9).

*Behold, the eye of the Lord is on those who fear Him,
on those who hope for His lovingkindness, to deliver
their soul from death, and to keep them alive in famine.*

Psalm 33:18,19

Our God, the omniscient, omnipresent, omnipotent One wants us to come to know the splendor of His majesty so we can worship Him. Freely. Joyfully. Wholeheartedly. For, as John Piper said, "Worship is a way of gladly reflecting back to God the radiance of His worth."[20] In the next chapter, let's reach back thousands of years and discover more evidence in our case for worship. The findings may astound you.

FIRE-SEEKER'S COMPANION
Questions for Group Interaction
or Individual Reflection

1. Getting to know God is different from knowing anyone else. How? What does the name *Elohim* tell you about God? *El Shaddai* reveals a new facet of God in contrast with *Elohim*. Explain how this applies to you.

2. Who gave God the name *Jehovah-jireh?* Describe the circumstances and what that name means to you. Who named God *Jehovah-nissi* and why? How does this affect your life?

3. *Jehovah-rophe* is another name for God. How did it come about? What does it say to you? Who gave God the name *Jehovah-shalom?* What led him to describe God this way? Does it apply to your circumstances?

4. *Jehovah-tsidkenu* means what? Who called God that and what was he prophesying with the name? What outward sign did God want from His people to show they knew Him as *Jehovah-m'kaddesh?* Is God saying anything to you through this name?

5. Who received the revelation of *Jehovah-shammah* and under what circumstances? How does that affect you? What does *Jehovah-rohi* mean? Who called God that and what does that tell you about Him for today?

6. Describe the scene when a servant of God named Him *Jehovah-sabaoth.* Apply that magnificent truth to your life right now. How does it make you feel?

7. In spite of God's many names, He is still one God, a Trinity. What is each member of the Trinity called? Name as many functions of each as you can. How do they interrelate to one another?

OPEN SHARING: FEEL FREE TO DISCUSS QUESTIONS OR ANYTHING RELATED TO THE CHAPTER THAT MINISTERED TO MEMBERS OF THE GROUP. LET THE HOLY SPIRIT LEAD YOU.

Fire-starter's Preparation
("Lab" Exercise)

Spend time alone and together worshipping the Lord. Before and after, record your thoughts and feelings in a journal. Write down changes you notice in your life.

NOTES

_____

_____

_____

_____

_____

_____

_____

_____

_____

_____

_____

_____

_____

_____

_____

_____

_____

_____

_____

_____

_____

Chapter Six

Of Tabernacles and Temples

 ave you ever gone prospecting for gold? I haven't, either. But thousands of fortune hunters throughout history have abandoned homes and families, rushed to remote areas of the world, and risked life and limb—all in search of this cherished mineral. From what I've read, a prospector has to be quite patient and intent on striking genuine treasure. Why? Because the valuable mineral often comes attached to and buried under other less glamorous materials. Miners expend tremendous energy excavating tons of rock. . .just to find a few ounces of gold.

If prospectors go to major extremes to unearth a shiny metal, shouldn't we apprentice worshippers be willing to dig a little to discover valuable tidbits about God? No book on worship would be quite complete without a look at the setting for Old Testament worship. Many of us have missed precious gems in

the Word by assuming that sections of the Old Testament contain an unending list of needless information. Although God's
manner of dealing with man *has* changed somewhat throughout
history, His principles remain unchanged by time.

How about if we approach the ancient tabernacle with the
attitude of one seeking buried treasure? Even the minute details,
in the way they foreshadow the Messiah, serve to confirm the
perfection of God. The precise directions for the construction
of the tabernacle in the wilderness, which God gave to Moses
so many thousands of years ago, contain a wealth of information. Hidden in the tabernacle lie secrets of God's plan for man
throughout the ages. We'll find insight as to how we, temples
of the living God, should conduct ourselves as worshippers.
John MacArthur cautioned,

> Worship is not giddy. It does not rush into God's
> presence unprepared and insensitive to His majesty.
> It is not shallow, superficial, or flippant. Worship is life
> lived in the presence of an infinitely righteous and om-
> nipresent God by one utterly aware of His holiness and
> consequently overwhelmed with his own unholiness.[21]

What does it mean to be "living temples?" The life-
changing truths in the ancient tabernacle will help us to answer
this question. As a springboard, we'll describe this old covenant place of worship. (Each detail has special significance, so
bear with us as we proceed slowly through this section).

The Lord called for the tabernacle of the congregation, or
tent of meeting, to be situated in a strategic way among the
twelve tribes. Numbers 2:2 records the precise order,

> *"The sons of Israel shall camp, each by his own
> standard, with the banners of their fathers' house-
> holds; they shall camp around the tent of meeting at
> a distance."*

God gave instructions for the tribes of Judah, Issachar and
Zebulun to camp on the east side; on the south side, the tribes
of Reuben, Simeon, and Gad. On the west side, the tribes of

Ephraim, Manasseh, and Benjamin, while Dan, Asher and Naphtali completed the arrangement on the north side. They erected the tabernacle, then, at the very center of the encampment. Only the sons of Aaron and the Levites, those set aside to minister to God, could set up camp *near* the tabernacle.

Like the hub of a wheel with spokes radiating outward, this tribal arrangement around the tabernacle made some dramatic statements. "Keep worship at the center of life! Revolve the rest of your life around it." That applies to us today, too. We often try to squeeze God into our schedules as an afterthought.

However, the Israelites had to place their personal tents far away from the tabernacle. The priests and Levites alone lived within a close proximity. This symbolized the covenant relationship that God established with His people for that period—He allowed only those in the priesthood to come into His presence. Organizing the camp around the tabernacle offered another advantage. Everyone could see it with an unobstructed view whenever Moses went in to meet with God,

> *And it came about, whenever Moses entered the tent, that all the people would arise and stand, each at the entrance of his tent and gaze after Moses until he entered the tent. And it came about, whenever Moses entered the tent, the pillar of cloud would descend and stand at the entrance of the tent and the Lord would speak with Moses. When all the people saw the pillar of cloud standing at the entrance of the tent, all the people would arise and worship, each at the entrance of his tent.*

> Exodus 33:8-10

When the pillar of cloud lifted, the Israelites could see a white linen fence-like enclosure and the badger skin covering the roof, visible above the fence. The only entrance opened into the east side of the outer fence. Over this gate hung curtains of blue, purple, scarlet and white linen. Passing through the gate and entering the courtyard, they encountered three distinct objects: the laver, the brazen altar and the tabernacle itself. Before entering the house of God, the priests washed up in the laver, a large brass basin located just outside the door of the tabernacle,

> "And Aaron and his sons shall wash their hands and their feet from it; when they enter the tent of meeting, they shall wash with water, that they may not die; or when they approach the altar to minister, by offering up in smoke a fire sacrifice to the Lord. So they shall wash their hands and their feet, that they may not die; and it shall be a perpetual statute for them, for Aaron, and his descendants throughout their generations."
>
> Exodus 30:19-21

Adjacent to the laver stood the altar of sacrifice. As we just read, the priests had to be clean before they could offer any sacrifices. The penalty for failing to obey? Death. Both the altar and the laver were constructed of brass, the laver solid, while the altar was made of shittim wood overlaid with brass.

Four distinct layers of materials formed a tent-like roof on the tabernacle. Its innermost layer consisted of curtains of fine white linen, blue, purple and scarlet. Eleven curtains of goats' hair covered this multicolored fabric. The next layer was a covering of rams' skins dyed red and finally, an outer covering of plain badger skins. Craftsmen made the walls of shittim wood and overlaid it with gold on the side facing inward. The door was made of hangings of white, blue, purple and scarlet, supported by five shittim wood posts overlaid with gold and sitting on a base of brass.

Just inside the tabernacle in the holy place were three objects: one directly ahead, one to the left, and one to the right. On the left stood a candlestick made of one solid piece of beaten gold, from which emanated all the light in the holy place,

"Then you shall make a lampstand of pure gold. The lampstand and its base and its shaft are to be made of hammered work; its cups, its bulb and its flowers shall be of one piece with it. And six branches shall go out from its sides, three branches of the lampstand from its one side, and three branches of the lampstand from its other side. Then you shall make its lamps seven in number, and they shall mount its lamps so as to shed light on the space in front of it."

Exodus 25:31-32,37

On the right side of the room was the second object, the table of showbread constructed of shittim wood overlaid with pure gold. The priests kept bread on it continually before the Lord. The third object in the holy place was the altar of incense, again of shittim wood covered with pure gold. On this altar the priests burned special incense each morning as a sweet smell unto the Lord.

Directly behind the altar of incense hung a veil that separated the holy place from the most holy place (holy of holies). The same four colors used in other curtains (blue, purple, scarlet and white), comprised this veil. In the most holy place the priest placed a solitary object, the ark of the covenant. Constructed also of shittim wood covered inside and out with pure gold, the ark looked like a gleaming chest. On top of the ark was the mercy seat made of one solid piece of pure gold. Two cherubim with their wings outstretched and their faces looking toward one another stood on the mercy seat.

That completes our brief "tour" of the tabernacle. Didn't God lay out precise instructions for the children of Israel to build a meeting place for Him? Let's take a closer look at the rich symbolism.

Each of the four colors in the curtains and wall hangings highlighted a specific aspect of the character and work of Jesus. White symbolized purity. It pointed toward the holy life He lived as the God-man on earth. Blue announced Jesus as the High Priest and purple testified of His Kingship. The fourth color, scarlet, revealed Him as the Suffering Savior.

From the symbolism of these four colors, we can see why the color white made up the outer enclosure. If anyone would gaze at the visible characteristics and behavior of Jesus, they could appreciate His very human, yet perfect life. Absolute purity distinguished Him from every other human being. Yet, worshippers may follow in His footsteps by depending on His Spirit. Qualities of purity and holiness in *us* draw people to Jesus.

What lay beyond the white enclosure, unnoticeable from a casual glance, spoke of a miracle: Emmanuel. God with us. An Israelite who approached the tabernacle would come upon a gate of multicolored curtains. It represented the Lord Jesus as the only way into God's presence. Remember His own Words, *"I am the Way, the Truth, and the Life. . . "* and *"I am the Door of the sheepfold."* We pass through this gate, in essence, when we accept Him as our personal Shepherd and Savior.

Being born again releases a supernatural joy into our lives. Delivered from the destruction of sin to the solid rock of faith, we *can* rejoice just like King David. He so relished God's presence, he said he would rather spend one day in the courtyard than a thousand days outside (Psalm 84:10).

For a Christian, life within the enclosure of the "courtyard" takes on new meaning from life without. Joy permeates seven steps essential to the life of the new-born worshipper. Since we are only just beginning to unravel the symbolism of the tabernacle, Psalm 100 does shed more light on the role of praise, the predecessor to worship in the holy of holies:

1. Shout joyfully.
2. Serve with gladness.
3. Come with joyful singing.
4. Know our God who made us.
5. Enter His gates with thanksgiving.
6. Enter His courts with praise.
7. Give thanks and bless His name.

Why? *For the Lord is good; His lovingkindness is ever-lasting, and His faithfulness to all generations.*

The first two commands characterize our daily walk with the Lord—to let everyone see our joy and willingness to serve Him. Singing, the third command, prepares us to come before the Lord in worship. The Israelites did this as they went to the tabernacle in the wilderness, and later, as they went to the temple in Jerusalem. Along the way, they praised God on instruments and with uplifted voices.

Once at the place of worship, the next two commands come into play. We need a reminder of who we're worshipping: Father and Son in all their wondrous glory. God is our Maker; we are His. Next, the psalmist urges us again to come singing our thanks and praise. The seventh command is to be grateful for having been in the presence of our God and to bless His name because of His great goodness.

These seven commands, or keys, pertain to us today as much as to the Hebrews—even more so now that *we* have become living temples. At the moment we accept Jesus as Lord and Savior, we pass from death to life, and as we mentioned, symbolically we move into the outer enclosure. However, many Christians remain in the courtyard for the rest of their lives. Satisfied and smug with salvation, they fail to pursue God fervently enough to enter the holy place and ultimately, the holy of holies.

Since the Lord has even allowed us to enter the courtyard, we have plenty of reasons to be full of jubilant praise and thanksgiving. These acts of obedience will lead us on to the lifestyle of true worship we desire. In fact, praise is such an important preface to worship that we'll include one more song by the "sweet psalmist of Israel." Psalm 150 begins and ends with the command to praise, and in between, tells us where, why, how and who should praise the Lord,

Praise the Lord!

Praise God in His sanctuary;

Praise Him in His mighty expanse.

Praise Him for His mighty deeds;

Praise Him according to His excellent greatness.

Praise Him with trumpet sound;

Praise Him with harp and lyre;

Praise Him with timbrel and dancing;

Praise Him with stringed instruments and pipe.

Praise Him with loud cymbals;

Praise Him with resounding cymbals;

Let everything that has breath praise the Lord.

Praise the Lord!

Now back to the rest of the ancient tabernacle. Having entered the gate, the priests stopped next at the laver. When they washed their hands and feet in that basin of highly polished brass, they saw the reflection of their faces. *And he made the laver of brass, and the foot of it brass, from the mirrors of the serving women who served the doorway of the tent of meeting* (Exodus 38:8). The laver is a symbol of the Word of God, compared to a mirror in the book of James, *For if anyone is a hearer of the word and not a doer, he is like a man who looks at his natural face in a mirror; for once he has looked at himself and gone away, he has immediately forgotten what kind of person he was* (James 1:23).

The laver had a dual purpose. According to Judson Cornwall, it "offered a place of both self-inspection and self-purification, for the same basin that revealed defilement afforded the means to remove that contamination."[22] So does the Word of God! From the book of Ephesians we learn that the Word washes us, just as the priests washed themselves in the laver,

> *. . .that He might sanctify her, having cleansed her*
> *by the washing of water with the Word, that He might*
> *present to Himself the church in all her glory, having*
> *no spot or wrinkle or any such things; but that she*
> *should be holy and blameless.*
>
> Ephesians 5:26,27

Through a daily application of the Word to our lives, the Lord cleanses us from the ways of the world. As we let Him give us a good scrub, He will lead us to the next step—the brazen altar. The significance of the sacrificial altar can only be found in the Word, which explains why the laver came first in the tabernacle. Jewish priests placed offerings on the altar every morning and evening. These offerings foreshadowed the death of Jesus, the Lamb of God. They are also symbolic of God's requirements in each of our lives. A further study of the offerings and sacrifices will equip us with some useful insight as to what Jesus accomplished on the cross, as well as God's provision for us to enter His presence in worship.

The following valuable summary provides a key to the meaning of five separate offerings described in the book of Leviticus:

Burnt offering: *Surrender* of Christ for the world

Meal offering: *Service* of Christ in life

Peace offering: *Serenity* of Christ in life

Sin offering: *Substitute* of Christ for sin

Trespass offering: *Satisfaction* of Christ for demands of God[23]

In preparation for the Old Testament burnt offering, priests had to slaughter a healthy animal, sprinkle its blood on and around the altar, and then let the fire totally consume it as *a burnt sacrifice, an offering made by fire, of a sweet savor unto the Lord* (Leviticus 1:17). The burnt or ascending offering

symbolized Jesus' willingness to lay down His life as the perfect
sacrificial Lamb for the redemption of a lost world.

We also see the necessity of our *acceptance* of His act of
love, and a total consecration of our lives to Him. Our act of
surrender needs to be as voluntary as the Lord's. We offer
ourselves to Him at the moment of salvation and every day
thereafter for the rest of our lives. As true worshippers, we
dedicate ourselves to Him without compromise. Just as the
offering on the brazen altar was consumed by fire, so does the
Lord long to see our hearts passionately consumed with the
fire of love for Him.

The meal or grain offering was symbolic of the way Christ
gave Himself to the Father for the service of man. We can see
this in the description of the offering,

> *Now when anyone presents a grain offering as an
> offering to the Lord, his offering shall be of fine flour,
> and he shall pour oil on it and put frankincense on
> it. . .and the priest shall offer it up in smoke as its
> memorial portion on the altar, an offering by fire of
> a soothing aroma to the Lord.*
>
> Leviticus 2:1,2

Here, the use of *fine flour* symbolized Jesus as the Bread
of Life, untainted with sin, who had the fullness of the Holy Spirit
(oil) poured out upon Him. Frankincense had a bitter taste, but
a beautiful scent when burned. This was prophetic, giving us
insight into the bitter agony and humiliation that Jesus would
endure, as well as how His uncompromising obedience would
please the Father. Why? Because of the results.

Peace offerings, also called fellowship offerings, had their
own special purpose and they mean something for us, as well.

First, read part of the formalities,

> *Now if His offering is a sacrifice of peace offerings,
> if he is going to offer out of the herd, whether male
> or female, he shall offer it without defect before the*

Lord. Then Aaron's sons shall offer it up in smoke on the altar on the burnt offering, which is on the wood that is on the fire; it is an offering by fire of a soothing aroma to the Lord. . .Now as for the flesh of the sacrifice of his thanksgiving peace offerings, it shall be eaten on the day of his offering. . .

Leviticus 3:1,5; 7:15

A peace offering differed from others in that it couldn't stand alone. Notice how the priests had instructions to place it *on* the burnt offering instead of directly on the wood on the altar. That could be because peace offerings symbolized restored fellowship with God made possible for us only by the atoning sacrifice of Jesus. No acceptable sacrifice first, no peace. Hebrews could eat the offering in joyful celebration of forgiveness and renewed closeness with God. We can celebrate too!

The priests performed the sin offering every time someone broke one of God's laws.

. . .if a person sins unintentionally in any of the things which the Lord has commanded not to be done, and commits any of them, if the anointed priest sins so as to bring guilt on the people, then let him offer to the Lord a bull without defect . . .

Leviticus 4:2,3

The animal was killed in the same manner as the other offerings, but the priest only dipped one finger in the blood and then sprinkled it seven times in front of the veil of the sanctuary before he poured the rest of the blood around the altar. This act foreshadowed Jesus' substitutionary sacrifice for the sins of mankind through the crucifixion, as well as the *power* of the Lamb's blood as the only means of cleansing humanity from sin forever. Each of us needs forgiveness. Inherent in a few drops of Jesus' blood is enough power to grant that forgiveness and open the way for all believers to enter into God's presence.

The fifth offering, the trespass (guilt) offering, covered any sin against the Lord's holy things. In addition to the animal sacrifice, the offender paid a sum of money to the one who was offended or injured,

If a person acts unfaithfully and sins unintentionally against the Lord's holy things, then he shall bring his guilt offering to the Lord; a ram without defect from the flock, according to your valuation in silver by shekels, in terms of the shekel of the sanctuary, for a guilt offering, and it shall be forgiven him.

                                                    Leviticus 5:15

Jesus removed our guilt before a holy Father, for He is the one we offend by our sin. Even the unintentional variety is serious enough to have required an offering to atone for it in the Old Testament. Some people think they're not guilty of anything because they, unlike criminals, have never *purposely* done wrong. But this passage makes it clear that any sin is serious. The blood of Jesus not only takes away our guilt before the Father, it also eliminates constant *feelings* of guilt that hinder fellowship.

Offerings played an important role in the everyday activities of Old Testament Jews. Through such strict customs, they came to understand a recurring theme: *they could not purify themselves before God.* It took the shedding of blood from something apart from them. The need for animal sacrifices and offerings have passed away since the death of Jesus, but the underlying principle has not. A study of ancient offerings can lead us to appreciate more the costliness of sin and the tremen- dous penalty the Son of God already paid on our behalf. Sin bears a heavy price! It cost Jesus His very life.

Our own worship and offerings should cost us something, too. If they don't, are they really *sacrifices?* We're not implying we must work or punish ourselves so our sins can be forgiven. Jesus fulfilled this requirement once and for all by giving His life on the Cross. Only through the blood of Jesus (brazen altar), as revealed through the Word (laver), do we have access to the presence of God. If we accept this and follow in His footsteps of our own free will, we can pick up our crosses daily. Every fleshly desire gets crucified,

> *I urge you therefore, brethren, by the mercies of God, to present your bodies a living and holy sacrifice, acceptable to God, which is your spiritual service of worship.*
>
> Romans 12:1

Once the offerings were completed, the Israelite priest would be standing outside the door of the tabernacle itself. Before we enter, let's look at what the outside of the tabernacle had to say. The curtains of four colors again foretold Jesus in all His glory: Perfect Man, Priest, King and Savior.

Covering the beautiful, colored curtains were more curtains of woven goats' hair. As one can imagine, they would be rough-textured even after being woven together. This was symbolic of the lifestyle of Jesus. Rather than the pampered, genteel existence of kingly courts, He had the rough, earthy life of a carpenter and traveling preacher.

In the rams' skins dyed red resided the revelation of Jesus as the sacrificial Lamb. Badgers' skins as the outer covering pointed towards His portrait the prophet Isaiah would paint,

> *He had no stately form or majesty that we should look upon Him, nor appearance that we should be attracted to Him. He was despised and forsaken of men, a man of sorrows, and acquainted with grief; and like one from whom men hide their face, He was despised, and we did not esteem Him.*
>
> Isaiah 53:2,3

After enduring beating and whipping, then hanging on a cross to die slowly, Jesus' outward appearance must have been pretty awful. The truth of His glorious identity remained hidden beneath an unappealing exterior. Similarly, the ugly badger skins covering the tabernacle completely disguised the glory of the presence of God within.

Thus far, we've met Jesus as the Perfect Man (outer enclosure), and the Suffering Savior (brazen altar). If we are to come to know Him intimately as our High Priest and King, we must take the next step.

The door of the tabernacle differed from the gate in the outer enclosure. Five posts instead of four supported this opening, symbolizing the five-fold ministry that began with the infilling of the Holy Spirit on the day of Pentecost. The ministries of the apostle, prophet, evangelist, pastor and teacher lead us through the door and on to a deeper revelation of Jesus.

Pure gold covered the five posts, speaking of the purity that must be present in the lives of these servants. Brass bases indicate that they must be tried by the fire of suffering before they can lead. After God has proven and anointed them, they have the ability to bring people into His presence.

Inside the holy place one would come upon an awesome sight—wall to wall gold. This revealed the radiant purity of Jesus, as well the need for purity in the life of a worshipper. There in the holy place, only the golden lampstand with its seven lamps shed any light in the room. The source of light, the lampstand, symbolized our Lord, anointed with the fullness of the Holy Spirit, and the lamps represented seven attributes of that Spirit,

> And the spirit of the Lord will rest on Him, the spirit of wisdom and understanding, the spirit of counsel and strength, the spirit of knowledge and the fear of the Lord.
>
> Isaiah 11:2

Craftsmen hammered the lampstand into the proper shape from one solid piece of gold, and only pure, beaten olive oil could burn in it. Every morning and evening the priests cleaned and trimmed the lamps' wicks and added fresh oil to insure that the light would burn continually.

In this description, we find some clues that tell us how to become better vessels of the Spirit of God. Both the gold for the candlestick and the olive oil had to undergo some changes before they could produce light. Likewise, we surrender and let God mold us into shape, just as our Lord allowed Himself to be beaten for our transgressions. Jesus is the Light and He became the *Light of the world* (John 9:5), by obediently submitting to the Father.

Through the anointed ministry of the church, God shows us the way to the holy place. Inside, He leads us by the Light of the world, the Spirit of our Lord. The Spirit alone can guide us into the presence of God.

Directly across from the lampstand in the holy place stood the table of showbread. This again foreshadowed the Lord Jesus as the Bread of Life, whose body was broken for the world. The celebration of Holy Communion reminds us of His act of love. If we eat of the Bread, we will have eternal life,

> *"As the living Father sent Me, and I live because of the Father, so he who eats Me, he also shall live because of Me. This is the bread which came down out of heaven; not as the fathers ate, and died, he who eats this bread shall live forever."*
>
> John 6:57,58

The light from the lampstand illuminated the table of showbread in the holy place, just as the light of the Holy Spirit clarifies the bread of the Word. Whether we hear it in an anointed sermon during a worship service, or in our personal devotions, only the *Spirit-enlightened* Word sustains us and renews our minds.

The third object in the holy place was the golden altar of incense, located directly before the veil that separated the holy place from the most holy place. Every morning and evening, as the priests filled the lamps with oil, they burned incense upon this altar. For those of us who want to be true worshippers and to come into the Lord's presence, this step bears utmost importance.

Once again, the gold altar signifies God's requirement for purity and holiness because of His own nature. *Thine eyes are too pure to approve evil, and Thou canst not look on wickedness with favor* (Habakkuk 1:13). Before the incense could become a sweet-smelling aroma, the priests had to place it on a pure base. So it goes in our lives. The incense of pleasing worship to God emanates from a pure heart.

Indicative of the costliness of worshipping *in the beauty of holiness* (Psalm 96:9), priests carefully prepared incense for use in the tabernacle only. Three spices—stacte, onycha and galbanum, combined in equal measure with frankincense and then tempered together by heating—comprised the special formula. After the priests evenly blended the ingredients into one, they crushed it into pieces suitable for burning before the Lord. Finally, only as fire consumed it, did the incense release its heavenly scent. For our worship to be sweet to God, we must also undergo the same preparation.

According to A.P. Gibbs, four characteristics comprise a worshipper's heart. They seem to correlate to the four ingredients of the incense. The first heart element? Remembrance—focusing on the Person and works of Jesus Christ. Then, gratitude. Reverence. And finally, awe. These four parts undergo the same gentle tempering process as the Hebrews' incense. Too little or too much heat will destroy the elements rather than blend them together. The Holy Spirit, though, knows the exact temperature required to remove all the impurities in every believer.

After the Lord perfectly tempers our hearts, we're ready to begin the next step. Whereas the heating and blending may have been a bit unpleasant, this step can be downright painful.

But when we consider what the Lord endured to open the way for us into His presence, we have no right to expect total exemption from discomfort.

Priests beat the blended incense into small pieces before they burned it. In the Hebrew language, the word translated "beaten" can be best expressed as "crushed" or "pulverized." The same applies to us. But we have already offered our bodies as living sacrifices in the outer court, and our soulish intellect and emotions for His enlightening in the holy place. In which part of our beings, then, does the "crushing" take place?

Still in the holy place of the soul where our stubborn will resides. It needs to undergo an intense refining process. Our every desire must conform to God's purpose for us. We give up our "rights" to have our own way. Once we voluntarily commit our lives to God, we relinquish complete control to Him. He becomes "Boss." Results of the crushing of our old nature far outweigh any temporary pain. Our worship will rise as a pleasing aroma to the Father. As it is written, *The sacrifices of God are a broken spirit; a broken and a contrite heart, O God, Thou wilt not despise* (Psalm 51:17). He achieves this brokenness by divine fire in the same way the priests lit the incense.

So first He consecrates our bodies, then our souls, and finally our spirits to Himself. The Lord Jesus underwent such an experience during His agony on the cross, as evidenced by His last words, *And Jesus, crying out with a loud voice, said, "Father, into Thy hands I commit My spirit." And having said this, He breathed His last* (Luke 23:46).

When we, like Jesus, place our spirits into the hands of the Father, allowing Him to consume us by the fire of the Holy Spirit, we are prepared to enter into His presence. The perfumed smoke from the burning incense rose toward the four-colored ceiling of the ancient tabernacle. So our gaze, no longer looking straight ahead, fixes heavenward on the Lord in all His glory— Perfect Man, Suffering Savior, Great High Priest and King of Kings.

The arrangement of the three objects in the holy place (golden lampstand, table of showbread and golden altar of incense) form points of an imaginary triangle. This relates in a significant way to the love of God triangle we studied earlier (knowledge, covenant and worship). From the illustration, we can see that each of the points "reflects" to the opposite side. By the light of the Holy Spirit (lampstand), we grow in intimate *knowledge* of our Lord. As we eat the bread of the Word (table of showbread) our *covenant* with Him deepens. Fervent worship (altar of incense) releases a sweet fragrance toward heaven.

When we have come to know God intimately through Jesus Christ and have entered into a committed covenant with Him; when the fire of worship consumes us, then He will lead us through the veil into the most holy place—the holy of holies.

Earlier we read that Jesus paved the way for us to pass through the veil and into the Father's presence. Now, because we have followed in the Lord's steps and have been prepared by the Spirit, we are ready to commune with God. Our great High Priest ushers us into the presence of the Almighty, much like the ancient high priest entered the most holy place to stand before the ark.

Under the old covenant God allowed only the high priest to enter the most holy place, and even then, but once a year to make atonement for the sins of the children of Israel. When he went in, he had to observe every single command and regulation. Any breach whatsoever would cost the priest his life. The Lord directed him to bring incense with him and set it in a specific place,

> *"And he shall take a firepan full of coals of fire from upon the altar before the Lord, and two handfuls of finely ground sweet incense and bring it inside the*

veil. And he shall put the incense on the fire before the Lord, that the cloud of incense may cover the mercy seat that is on the ark of the testimony, lest he die."

Leviticus 16:12,13

We have already seen one implication of the incense and now we find another. In Psalm 141 and in the book of the Revelation, incense represents the prayers of God's people ascending to heaven, *May my prayer be counted as incense before Thee; the lifting up of my hands as the evening offering* (Psalm 141:2).

And when He had taken the book, the four living creatures and the twenty-four elders fell down before the Lamb, having each one a harp, and golden bowls, full of incense, which are the prayers of the saints.

Revelation 5:8

You may remember that the sole object in the most holy place was the ark of the covenant with the mercy seat and cherubim on top of it. Not even a ray of light detracted from the glory of the Lord in that room. Two cherubim facing each other with outstretched wings stood as silent witnesses of God's grandeur in heaven and on earth. The mercy seat reminds us that only God's infinite grace made a way for us to come and commune with Him. We could never earn that privilege based on our own merit.

"And there I will meet with you; and from above the mercy seat, from between the two cherubim which are upon the ark of the testimony, I will speak to you about all that I will give you in commandment for the sons of Israel."

Exodus 25:22

What did the priests store inside the chest-like ark? The stone tablets with the Ten Commandments, a pot of manna and the rod of Aaron. These objects also bore witness to divine miracles and foreshadowed a new covenant in Jesus Christ. The stone tablets indicated the inflexible law that God gave Moses, and the rigid manner in which He dealt with man in the Old Testament. Breaking His laws bore fatal consequences, but Jesus *fulfilled the law.* In the manna we can uncover another reference to Jesus as the Bread of Life from heaven. What do we find in the rod of Aaron that speaks of our Lord?

First of all, the rod or stick verified the call of Aaron and his descendants to the priesthood. God confirmed His choice of a spiritual leader when He caused buds to form on a dead branch that belonged to Aaron. This again prophesied of Jesus as the great High Priest who would miraculously rise from the dead, and as the One who would bring new spiritual life to those who had been dead in sin. Even further, the rod spoke of the restoration of the twelve tribes of Israel that will occur during the great tribulation. Although the Israelites suffered spiritual death when they rejected Jesus, they won't stay in that condition forever. New life will spring forth from that which seems dead.

The entire tabernacle illustrated the scope of God's dealings with man through the ages, and confirmed at least three important facts: First, *Jesus Christ is the same yesterday and today, yes and forever* (Hebrews 13:8). Second, God has always desired and planned for man to enjoy close fellowship with Him. And third, all that Satan stole from Adam, Jesus bought back for both Jews and Gentiles, now and forever. In Him, old and new merge to complete the restoration of our relationship with the Father.

What a great God we serve! As true worshippers, He calls us to come apart and be separate from the world, rather than letting it ensnare us in its hustle and bustle. Then our lives will exemplify, even at first glance, the transforming power of God's love. Evidence of our assignment as "temples of the Holy Spirit" will be as obvious as the glory cloud over the ancient Hebrew tabernacle. Stay with us for the next chapter, and you'll find out more about how to make that a personal reality.

FIRE-SEEKER'S COMPANION
Questions for Group Interaction
or Individual Reflection

1. Why study the details of the ancient Hebrew tabernacle? Why do you think more Christians don't take time to learn about it?

2. Where did the tabernacle stand in relation to the rest of the Israelites' wilderness camp? Who could pitch their tents near it and who had to remain at a distance? What does this arrangement say about worship today?

3. What enclosed the courtyard of the tabernacle and what does it mean? What four colors did they use for curtains at the gate and what do those colors symbolize? Going into the courtyard symbolizes what experience in the life of a believer? What does he learn to do there?

4. Describe the laver—what the Israelites used it for and what it means to you. Do the same for the brazen altar. Why the laver before the altar? What covered the exterior of the tabernacle and why?

5. What three objects stood in the holy place and what do they symbolize?

6. Describe the most holy place. What does each have to do with you today?

7. How do you get into the most holy place where you can truly worship the living God? Why do you want to be able to enter into that sanctuary?

OPEN SHARING: FEEL FREE TO DISCUSS QUESTIONS OR ANYTHING RELATED TO THE CHAPTER THAT MINISTERED TO MEMBERS OF THE GROUP. LET THE HOLY SPIRIT LEAD YOU.

FIRE-STARTER'S PREPARATION
("Lab" Exercise)

SPEND TIME ALONE AND TOGETHER WORSHIPPING THE LORD.
BEFORE AND AFTER, RECORD YOUR THOUGHTS AND FEELINGS IN A
JOURNAL. WRITE DOWN CHANGES YOU NOTICE IN YOUR LIFE.

NOTES

Chapter Seven

Prayer: The Heartbeat of Worship

rayer cannot be successfully separated from worship, for it prepares the soul for worship, expresses the spirit in worship and interacts with God, which is worship. Worship without prayer is like daytime without light, a school without students, a choir without music, or an automobile without fuel. . . The praying saint cannot keep from worshipping; the prayerless saint cannot rise to worship.[24]

Prayer is the mold in which the character of our life is shaped.[25]

Prayer is the sap of the vineyard. When it flows, life will manifest itself, but when it ceases to flow, the leaves brown and fall off, the fruit withers on the vine, and the plant goes into the dormant stage. Prayer is therefore not elective but essential: no prayer—no life flow; no life flow—no fruit.[26]

Prayer *must* have priority. Prayer *must* be our bolt to lock up the night, our key to open the day.[27]

I guess we'd better get serious about prayer if we want a lifestyle of worship. Our goal is to practice the presence of God and maintain constant communion with Him. In the Apostle Paul's letter to the church at Colossae, he wrote, **Devote** *yourselves to prayer, keeping alert in it with an attitude of thanksgiving* (Colossians 4:2). During the Lord's time of trial in the garden of Gethsemane, He asked the disciples to pray. What did they do? They all fell asleep,

> . . .*So, you men could not keep watch with Me for one hour? Keep watching and praying, that you may not enter into temptation; the spirit is willing, but the flesh is weak.*
>
> Matthew 26:40-41

No matter how strong the human spirit may be, as long as we're housed in earthly temples, we'll struggle to overcome the weaknesses of the flesh. But we can emerge victorious through watchful prayer. The disciples failed to pray and look what happened to them. They scattered throughout the area. Peter even went so far as to deny the Lord, not once, but three times.

True worshippers learn to be prayer warriors. We can't expect to "sleep," as Jesus called it, all week long, and then run to church on Sunday to find the presence of God. Why wait? We can commune with Him every day.

Let me give you at least three very good reasons to pray. First and foremost: it brings honor to God. "Prayer is an act of worship, a paying homage" to our Father in heaven.[28]

Secondly, prayer develops humility by bringing us to the point of total dependence upon God. Continuing in prayer will lead us to the realization that, without Him, we can do nothing of lasting value. Paul summed up this thought in his letter to the Roman church when he wrote, *For I know that nothing good dwells in me, that is, in my flesh; for the wishing is present in me, but the doing of good is not* (Romans 7:18). Paul recognized his helplessness without God. So too, will every true worshipper discover as he learns to pray.

The third reason for prayer? So that we may receive what we need from God, for the Lord Himself, declared,

> *"Ask, and it shall be given you; seek and you shall find; knock, and it shall be opened to you. For everyone who asks receives, and he who seeks, finds, and to him who knocks it shall be opened."*
>
> Matthew 7:7,8

We don't mean to promote God as a kind of divine "Santa Claus" who grants us every single request. He gives us what we need, in line with His character. When we petition the Father in the name of Jesus, we pray for those same things He desires to give us, as outlined in His Word. We could say, in a sense, that we're "praying for God."

This may sound a bit unorthodox at first. But think about it. Prayer involves agreeing with God. We direct our prayers towards the accomplishment of His purposes in this world. He wants *everyone* to know Him. How often do we find our prayer time all but consumed with concerns for family, friends and finances? Along with personal needs, we can pray that leaders, both among God's people and in the world, would be open to His Holy Spirit. The Apostle Paul wrote about this to Timothy, his young helper,

> *First of all, then, I urge that entreaties and prayers, petitions and thanksgivings, be made on behalf of*

all men. For kings and all who are in authority, in order that we may lead a tranquil and quiet life in all godliness and dignity.

I Timothy 2:1,2

We can agree with God in prayer that He would show Himself strong on behalf of His people, that He alone would reign supreme in the kingdom of our hearts. One man named George Mueller dedicated his life to helping orphaned children in England. Knowing that God had called him to that particular ministry, he depended entirely upon His support. George never asked for money. He relied on prayer and developed the following daily prayer vigil.

Each day he read his Bible with expectation until he came upon something especially meaningful. He always read believing that God would give Him a specific word for the day. When He did, George wrote down what it meant to him. Then he meditated on the significance of the Scriptures and examined his thoughts, allowing the Holy Spirit to bring *His* ultimate purpose into focus. Finally, he spoke to someone about what he learned and how it related to him.

During his lifetime, George Mueller became accustomed to starting each day in this way. If you haven't already discovered the benefits, you might consider developing similar habits. (We'll show you more about how to put these and other ideas into practice in the following section "A Day by Day Lifestyle.")

Worshipful prayer goes beyond a mere morning routine. The Lord would like to guide our every step throughout the day, if we would listen to Him. Watching and praying enable us to hear His voice clearly. He has given every child of His the Holy Spirit to help in this area. During times of prayer we, like George Mueller, receive guidance and direction that will keep us firmly in the center of God's will.

Another praying saint, Thomas Aquinas, noted that persistence in prayer consisted not of asking for many things, but of desiring *one* thing. God Himself. This steadfastness brings about change in every parameter of our existence. Sincere prayer, based on God's Word and led by His Spirit, builds character. It establishes order in a once-fragmented life because God is the author of order, not confusion.

Prayer exerts unbelievable demands on us. We might reach a stage where we'll have to decide to venture forth into uncharted territory. As we open our hearts and allow the Lord freedom, He will develop us in ways far beyond anything we, on our own, have ever attempted. True, worshipful prayer transcends the structure of ingrained behavior and rigid church traditions. In prayer we can experience the holy and compassionate heart of the Lord.

C.H. Spurgeon once asked,

Why is it that some people are often in a place of worship and yet they're not holy? It is because they neglect their (prayer) closets. They love the wheat but they do not grind it; they would have the corn but they will not go forth into the field to gather it; the fruit hangs on the tree but they will not pluck it; and the water flows at their feet but they'll not stoop to drink it. (*Source Unknown*)

Achieving communion with the God of the universe is the essence and goal of worship. We can't hurry the process or neglect it. But realistically, how often in our daily routines do we find ourselves so caught up in the affairs of living...that we squeeze in a few quick moments with the Lord? Those times when I'm too driven to pray, the "wheel falls off my race car," so to speak. Soon, I'm spinning toward a crash. Life ceases to be a joy.

We would do well to pursue our many interests only to the degree that we can stay relaxed. No more. When we pray and work, or pray and participate in sports, or pray and make love, all at a pleasant pace, life is great. Living like that prevents us from getting caught on the endless merry-go-round of obligations.

❧

"But committed Christians should roll up their shirt sleeves. We should work hard," you might be thinking. True, we should. In fact, Chuck Colson and Jack Eckerd wrote a great book on the subject entitled, **Why America Doesn't Work.** Pushed to the extreme, though, we can easily fall into the "Martha Syndrome." She was doing important household tasks, but she missed the most crucial moments of all. Her industriousness kept her from resting at the feet of the Master to bask in His love.

A study of the meditative lifestyles of true worshippers reveals the ample time they set aside to live close to God, and to listen for rhema (specific word) from Him. They have learned to obey the command to *be still and know that I am God* (Psalm 46:10). John Wesley, a devout saint, described how he was able to achieve this, "Though I am always in haste, I am never in a hurry because I never undertake more work than I can go through with calmness of spirit."

How do we continue in prayer, or, as the Scriptures read, *pray without ceasing* (I Thessalonians 5:17)? First, by maintaining that open door we have received through the blood of Jesus. The lifestyle of worship is a life of forgiveness, even as the Lord forgives us—unconditionally. No unconfessed sin. No unforgiveness. We depend on Him to help us forgive every offense against us, whether real or imagined. In His sermon on the mount, Jesus told His followers, *"But I say to you, love your enemies, and pray for those who persecute you"* (Matthew 5:44).

Motives in prayer are important to God. Selfish motives or prayers out of line with the Word fall short. A.W. Pink, in his lecture on the matter of scriptural prayer, wrote,

> *The promises of God contain the matter of prayer and define the measure of it. . . Hence, the better we are acquainted with the Divine promises, and the more we are enabled to understand the goodness, grace and mercy prepared and proposed in them, the better equipped we are for acceptable prayer.*[29]

That may explain why some (not all) prayers go unanswered. Praying God's promises insures victory—eventually. Would you like to be a success as a prayer warrior? For all who answer "yes," He prescribed a formula to Joshua as he was preparing to lead the Israelites into the Promised Land,

> *This book of the law shall not depart from your mouth, but you shall **meditate** on it day and night, so that you may be careful to do according to all that is written in it; for then you will make your way prosperous, and then you will have success.*
>
> Joshua 1:8

God commands us, along with Joshua, to learn His Word and speak it in prayer to receive His blessings. Then we'll be able to pray with the great expectation of His power being demonstrated in, through and for us. Mouthing words or putting on the appearance of holiness with no inner transformation gets us nowhere. God knows the desires of our heart and He wants us to hunger after His presence (Jeremiah 29:13).

A.W. Pink's mother taught him the following poem. How well these few simple lines express the need for sincerity,

> I often say my prayers,
> But do I ever pray?
> And do the wishes of my heart
> Go with the words I say?
> I may as well kneel down
> And worship gods of stone,
> As offer to the living God
> A prayer of words alone.[30]

"A life formed by prayer is a life opposed to illusion, self-deception, and hypocrisy . . . prayer is at war with falsehood."[31] These inward attitudes play a premier role in our ability to worship. Time after time in the Scriptures, we find our Lord confronting the pious appearances of religious leaders. In the twenty-third chapter of Matthew, He told them in no uncertain terms,

> *"Woe to you, scribes and Pharisees, hypocrites! For you clean the outside of the cup and of the dish, but inside they are full of robbery and self-indulgence. You blind Pharisees, first clean the inside of the cup and of the dish, so that the outside of it may become clean also. For you are like whitewashed tombs which on the outside appear beautiful, but inside they are full of dead men's bones and all uncleanness. Even so you too outwardly appear righteous to men, but inwardly you are full of hypocrisy and lawlessness."*
>
> Matthew 23:25-28

Hardly words of blessing. Jesus spoke for the Father: He wants hearts of loving obedience, not showy outward displays. His rebuke serves only to re-emphasize the Lord's concern over our inner condition. We find in the book of Hosea another brief synopsis of God's priorities, *"For I delight in loyalty rather than sacrifice, and in the knowledge of God rather than burnt offerings"* (Hosea 6:6).

What does all this have to do with us today? We don't try to offer burnt offerings anymore. And though we may not consider ourselves as hypocritical as the Pharisees, we who have become "living temples of the Holy Spirit" still need regular cleaning. Just as Jesus drove out the unclean activities from the earthly temple in Jerusalem (designed as a house of prayer—Luke 19:46), so He purges us. *For prayer, and through prayer.* If we allow Him, He will accomplish this in each one of us.

When our "house" becomes such a cleansed and praying vessel, we can enter into the conscious presence of God. . .to behold the glorious light of His countenance. . .and commune with Him at the mercy seat. Such joy and peace we experience there give us a tiny taste of all that awaits us in everlasting glory with Him.

❦

FIRE-SEEKER'S COMPANION
Questions for Group Interaction
or Individual Reflection

1. How do you feel about prayer? Does it have the importance in your life that the opening quotes emphasize?

2. What did the disciples do when Jesus asked them to pray during His hour of need? How long did He want them to pray? What happened to them when they failed to obey?

3. Why should you pray? Name as many reasons as you can.

4. What does "praying for God" mean? How does that differ from most people's prayers? How does it compare with yours?

5. Who was George Mueller and what made him stand out as a Christian? Name some other praying saints from history and some you know personally.

6. What are the keys to a meditative lifestyle?

7. When Jesus scolded the Pharisees, what did He say? How can you prevent that in your own life?

OPEN SHARING: FEEL FREE TO DISCUSS QUESTIONS OR ANYTHING RELATED TO THE CHAPTER THAT MINISTERED TO MEMBERS OF THE GROUP. LET THE HOLY SPIRIT LEAD YOU.

FIRE-STARTER'S PREPARATION
("Lab" Exercise)

SPEND TIME ALONE AND TOGETHER WORSHIPPING THE LORD. BEFORE AND AFTER, RECORD YOUR THOUGHTS AND FEELINGS IN A JOURNAL. WRITE DOWN CHANGES YOU NOTICE IN YOUR LIFE.

NOTES

_____

_____

_____

_____

_____

_____

_____

_____

_____

_____

_____

_____

_____

_____

_____

_____

_____

_____

PART THREE

ALL-CONSUMING FIRE

Chapter Eight

A Day by Day Lifestyle

ascination. Admiration. Adoration. Veneration. Communion. Natural responses to a supernatural God! We demonstrate worship in a variety of ways. Authors Allen & Borror remind us, "We are not simply spirit beings. We are more than hearts or souls or 'inner beings.' We are persons possessing an intricate complex of physical and spiritual realities."[32]

Judson Cornwall learned for himself the truth of this, especially in the realm of individual responses to God. After speaking at a convention, he led the people into a wonderful time of praise and worship. The Lord urged him to take note of what the people were doing as they rejoiced in His presence. Some stood. Some danced. Others sang. Each worshipped in his own way.

Without any human direction, the scene changed. Some who stood, lay prostrate before the Lord and some who danced knelt and wept. All followed the leading of God in their hearts. As Judson watched this taking place, he heard the Lord say to him,

> "The lesson I want you to learn is not to make people specialists in the expression of their worship. Allow for variety both corporately and individually. No one action can express all emotions, so allow for multiple actions in each person so that his or her worship can be complete."[33]

For easy reference we'll briefly summarize these avenues of expressing, in praise and worship, our love of God.

Voice:

> *I will bless the Lord at all times; His praise shall continually be in my mouth.*
>
> Psalm 34:1

> *Be glad in the Lord and rejoice you righteous ones, and shout for joy all you who are upright in heart.*
>
> Psalm 32:11

> *Praise the Lord in song, for He has done excellent things.*
>
> Isaiah 12:5

> *And they shall speak of the glory of Thy kingdom, and talk of Thy power.*
>
> Psalm 145:11

Silence:

> But the Lord is in His holy temple. Let all the earth be silent before Him.
>
> Habakkuk 2:20

Hands:

> I will bless Thee as long as I live; I will lift up my hands in Thy name.
>
> Psalm 63:4

> O clap your hands, all peoples; Shout to God with the voice of joy.
>
> Psalm 47:1

Body:

> Come let us worship and bow down; Let us kneel before the Lord our Maker. For He is our God.
>
> Psalm 95:6

> And with a leap, he stood upright and began to walk; and he entered the temple with them, walking and leaping and praising God.
>
> Acts 3:8

> Let them praise His name with dancing.
>
> Psalm 149:3

> Behold, bless the Lord, all servants of the Lord, who serve by night in the house of the Lord!
>
> Psalm 134:1

Instruments:

> *Praise Him with trumpet sound; Praise Him with*
> *harp and lyre. Praise Him with timbrel and danc-*
> *ing; Praise Him with stringed instruments and*
> *pipe. Praise Him with loud cymbals; Praise Him*
> *with resounding cymbals.*

Psalm 150:3-5

No matter which of these responses we use to praise and worship the Lord, thankful hearts and sacrificial spirits mean the most to Him. We don't worship to please men or "show off" to them, but as a way of giving honor to God.

How about if we investigate the lifestyle of a true worshipper in today's world? We've cited many *biblical* examples of those who enjoyed a close relationship with God, but because of their remoteness, we may have a hard time envisioning ourselves in their places. In order to see the practical application of these principles, let's assume a privileged vantage point from which to "view" a day in the life of one such twentieth-century worshipper. From there, what could we expect to observe?

Early in the morning, even long before the birds begin to greet the rising sun, Jake awakens. As he rubs the sleep from his eyes, he says in a hoarse voice, "Good morning, Lord. Thank you for one more day." During the next few moments as he throws off the covers, gets out of bed and takes care of personal needs, he hums a gentle hymn of praise. Removing his Bible from its familiar spot on the nightstand (placed carefully there the previous evening before he fell asleep), he pads into the kitchen for a glass of chilled fruit juice. Then, he's off to his favorite niche to spend precious moments with the Lord.

What began earlier as soft humming, now grows into joyful song. Holding his Bible close to his heart and walking back and forth, he expresses how thankful he is for all God has done: the sacrifice and resurrection of Jesus, the cleansing power of

His Blood, forgiveness, new life, freedom from the bondage of sin, and above all else, eternal life with Him.

Over the years, Jake has learned the blessings of openly sharing his feelings with the Lord. As his time of praise and gratitude continues, we see him clap occasionally, lift his hands, and wipe away tears. Then something happens. God once again fulfills His promise to *inhabit the praises of His people.*

In mid-stride, Jake comes to a standstill and stops singing. We can hear him whisper again and again the name of *Jesus.* In gentle reverence he lifts his hands, as if offering his very heart back to the Lord. The sweet communion he feels radiates through the tranquil glow on his face.

Slowly he kneels in front of the easy chair and lets his Bible fall open to the twenty-third Psalm. He reads the words in quiet affirmation of their truth. We hear him pray for his family (even Monarch), for his pastor and church leaders around the world, as well as for government leaders. His moving petitions flow forth—for their forgiveness and guidance—in each case according to the scriptural promises he knows by heart.

Last of all we hear him pray that he would be a better husband. A more faithful servant. A better steward of God's gifts. He asks that he would be able to see everything from God's perspective rather than his own. Can you sense the fervor with which he pleads to be conformed to the image of Jesus?

As he starts turning the well-worn pages of his Bible, we hear one last petition for himself, "Lord, open my eyes, so I can really see wonders out of your law. . .make your Word alive to me and feed me my daily bread." Reaching into the drawer of the nearby end table, he brings forth his Bible study notebook and pen. He is prepared to receive God's directions for the day.

For the next hour or so he seems unaware of the passage of time. He reads, occasionally nodding his head and smiling, and then as a truth is revealed, exclaims, "Thank you, Lord!". . .or "Hallelujah!". . .or "I praise You!" while he jots down a few lines in his notebook. Continuing in his daily Bible study, he moves to his desk, where, within easy reach are commentaries, a large concordance and a Bible dictionary. Surrounded by the ponderous volumes, he glances at his watch and breathes a sigh of contentment. He still has half an hour to research the priceless truths earlier revealed.

Time slips by, and much to his dismay, he must set aside his favorite texts until later. All too soon the moment arrives to get ready for the challenges of a day's work. Leaving the room, he sees his wife, Mary. She has just finished her time of personal devotions, and he greets her good morning with a warm kiss and embrace.

With his arms still around her, he catches her enthusiasm as she says, "Hon, I've got good news. I think the Lord has given us an answer. If you hurry up and get ready for work, we can talk about it over breakfast." Humming softly to herself, she heads into the kitchen while he busies himself getting dressed.

A short time later, his nose leads him to the source of the wonderful aroma wafting through the house. He wanders into the kitchen, Bible and notebook in one hand and jacket tossed casually over his shoulder. "Mmm. . .homemade muffins! Just what I wanted. How'd you know, sweetheart?"

She smiles and sets down a delicious breakfast before him and one at her own place. He takes her hand, they bow their heads, and he invites the Lord to bless the food.

Having finished his meal, he says, "That was great, hon. Sure am glad I married you. . ." Then he pauses. "Let's hear what the Lord showed you this morning. You're pretty excited about it."

"Well, I think we're supposed to go ahead and accept the pastor's offer. I feel right about it. The Lord seemed to be saying that *now* is the time for us to step out in faith."

Jumping up from her chair, she grabs the Bible, opens it and points to a verse. "Here is our answer."

He chuckles aloud as his eyes slowly scan the words. Then he stands up and gives her a big hug. "That's great, hon. Wait 'til I show you what the Lord told me this morning, too." He grins as he picks up his notebook. Then he leads her over to their favorite love seat, waits for her to sit down and puts his arm around her while opening the notebook on her lap. "Read this," he urges, indicating the passage.

She reads aloud, giving special emphasis to the words he had underlined, *Brethren, I count not myself to have apprehended; but this one thing I do, forgetting those things which are behind, and reaching forth unto those things which are before, I press toward the mark for the prize of the high calling of God in Christ Jesus...* She sets the notebook down and looks up at him with tears in her eyes. "That's...the exact verse...He gave me!"

"I know. The Lord sure is faithful. So it's settled then. We'll call Pastor this afternoon and tell him we'll be honored to lead praise and worship. Let's pray now. It's almost time for me to go." They clasp hands and begin to pray for each other, calling upon God's protection and blessing. Completing their special time together, they walk hand in hand to the front door for one last hug before he leaves for work.

As he pulls into the space marked "Maintenance Supervisor" in the employee parking lot, Jake pauses a moment, listening to the last strains of the praise music coming softly through the radio. Climbing out of the car, he grabs the card with his Scripture memory verse for the day and heads to his office. A co-worker awaiting their regular prayer group greets him with enthusiasm, "I really look forward to these few minutes we have before work. It sure makes a big difference."

Another worker wanders into the boiler room, and overhearing the conversation, adds, "Yeah, I don't know how we made it around here before."

Morning passes quickly. At noon he picks up his Bible and lunch box Mary packed for him and heads for his favorite dining spot out by the pond. It's so peaceful there with the ducks at play in the water. He smiles when he finds the love note tucked underneath his sandwich, and breathes a prayer of thanks for such a great companion. When he's done eating, he reads some Psalms and Proverbs and concentrates on his memory verse until the end of the lunch hour.

The afternoon poses a few minor crises for him, most of which he handles with calm efficiency—a composure resulting from the assurance that Someone far greater than himself is in control. It wasn't always that way. Time was, when he rushed off to work late, agitated and anxious about what problems the day would bring. How well he knows that Jesus does, indeed, make a difference. His grace is always sufficient (II Corinthians 12:9).

Afternoon rush hour traffic on the way home, enough to make anybody lose his temper, is no longer the harrowing, white-knuckled experience it used to be. Instead, Jake offers a "sacrifice of praise," singing familiar Scripture songs of victory. He looks forward to the fellowship he and his wife will have that evening with friends.

As he turns into their street, he hears the faint barking of a dog. At the driveway an exuberant bundle of four-legged energy meets him. "Monarch!" he exclaims. "Are you glad to be back from the vet, old boy? Sure missed you this morning!" Monarch continues to bark and run in circles, bounding and leaping about as he trots beside his master into the house. "Say, I've got to call the Pastor right away—tell him our decision. . . ."

Once inside, his sweetheart of twenty-five years greets him passionately and escorts him to his easy chair in the den. "Supper will be ready soon, hon, so just relax 'til then."

"Can you spare a moment to come sit with me while I make that call to Pastor? We're a team on this assignment, so you need to be here." His thoughtfulness elicits a grateful smile in response and she perches on the arm of his chair. Nearby, Monarch heaves a sigh of contentment.

A short while after dinner, surrounded by their friends, they excitedly share how God had spoken to them both that morning. They tell how, for the past week, they had been seeking guidance for a major decision. They had asked, and true to His Word, the Lord had given wisdom liberally. Knowing the responsibility involved in leading and teaching worship, they needed the assurance that it was, in fact, God's will for them.

Once the friends have gone home and just the three of them—Jake, Mary and Monarch—are alone again, they relax together. Husband and wife share the events of the day and enjoy one another's company. Opening a Bible one last time, they take turns reading aloud. Each offers insight into the passage and how they can apply it to their lives. Drawing to a close their time in the Word, they kneel down side by side to pray. As we leave our vantage point, we find Jake and Mary giving thanks for the blessing of their deepening walk with the Lord, and looking forward to miracles yet to come.

What can we discover from this story? It may serve as one example of our goal: to live life as a worshipper. Worship varies from day to day and from person to person, of course, so we don't mean to suggest rigidly imitating Jake and Mary. But scriptural dynamics emerge from the story that we can use as a guide. All the major elements of worship we've discussed thus far come together in one practical illustration.

In review: God's invitation to worship extends to all people. He doesn't play favorites. The main character was not anyone unusual—just an ordinary working man who loved the Lord. Most importantly, he kept God at the center of his whole life. When he got up early in the morning, his very first thoughts focused on the Lord.

Like the psalmist David, Jake had an obvious hunger to commune with God. He was more than willing to sacrifice a couple hours sleep to have enough time with Him. *O God, Thou art my God;* **early** *will I seek Thee: my soul* **thirsteth** *for Thee, my flesh* **longeth** *for Thee in a dry and thirsty land, where no water is* (Psalm 63:1). He freely expressed heart attitudes of humility and gratitude. Through songs of praise that led him into worship, he entered the sweet presence of the Holy Spirit. Although our worshipper enjoyed very close fellowship with the Lord, he still regarded Him with reverent awe.

He followed up his time of communion in song with Spirit-inspired prayer. Waiting patiently on the Lord, He prayed for the needs of others, for himself to be more like Jesus, and for God's will to be accomplished in the earth. He read the Word with expectation, knowing God would provide guidance for his life. Next, he proceeded on with joy to a more in-depth study of the Bible in all its intricate beauty. Our worshipper had discovered there a source of unending fulfillment. He valued the Word so much that he carried it to work with him, and even made out special cards with daily verses to memorize.

He shared deep love (nurtured by worship) with his cherished wife, and she followed his example in a commitment to early morning devotions. They each recognized that they were a gift, one to another, from the Father—their first love. Their lifestyle of worship gave birth to a desire to serve Him. As doors to ministry opened and God confirmed His will in that area, they stepped forward in faith. Their waiting showed not any hesitancy to serve, but an acknowledgment of their total dependence upon the Lord for their service to be fruitful. In fact, this interdependent relationship was evident throughout the day.

At work, Jake asked God to be in control. For years, he had led a prayer group with his co-workers where his simple faith shined as a light to those around him. It resulted in calmness of spirit in spite of the circumstances that confronted him. Also, the joy of the Lord in his heart gave him a deep appreciation for nature, God's creation. In the evening, he and his wife got together with close Christian friends to fellowship and encourage one another. Their day closed like it began—with prayer and the Word, but this time together as a family. *Evening, and morning, and at noon, will I pray, and cry aloud: and He shall hear my voice* (Psalm 55:17). *I will bless the Lord at all times; His praise shall continually be in my mouth* (Psalm 34:1).

Non-stop worship of our wonderful Lord! In any endeavor, practice makes perfect. As Judson Cornwall stated, "Worship is best learned by worshipping."[34] What begins with the seed of decision in our hearts and springs up to bud in the soil of everyday life, will come to full bloom as we find our place in congregational worship. Just as the bloom comes after the bud, so too, does worship in the assembly grow out of personal, daily worship. Allen and Borror expressed this thought beautifully,

> . . .**all of life becomes a worship service**. If Christians were devotedly practicing this lifestyle, a corporate service could not miss being a great blessing, for it would simply be a continuation of a worship service begun days (or weeks or months) before.[35]

FIRE-SEEKER'S COMPANION
Questions for Group Interaction
or Individual Reflection

1. Do all people worship God the same? Why or why not? How do you feel about that?

2. List as many ways to worship God as you can. Which ones are you most comfortable with and why? Which new ways would you be willing to try?

3. Describe the early-morning activities of our worshipper, Jake. Compare and contrast that with your own life. Do you need some improvement?

4. How did Jake apply his love of God to his work day? What can you do to worship God all day long?

5. Evening was a special time for Jake, too. Note some things he and his wife did that would help you in your walk with the Lord.

6. Individual worship during the week leads up to what event in the life of a believer? Why this natural progression?

7. What can you do, with God's help, to develop a lifestyle of worship? Are you willing to try? What results do you think you will see?

OPEN SHARING: FEEL FREE TO DISCUSS QUESTIONS OR ANYTHING RELATED TO THE CHAPTER THAT MINISTERED TO MEMBERS OF THE GROUP. LET THE HOLY SPIRIT LEAD YOU.

Fire-starter's Preparation
("Lab" Exercise)

SPEND TIME ALONE AND TOGETHER WORSHIPPING THE LORD. BEFORE AND AFTER, RECORD YOUR THOUGHTS AND FEELINGS IN A JOURNAL. WRITE DOWN CHANGES YOU NOTICE IN YOUR LIFE.

NOTES

_____

_____

_____

_____

_____

_____

_____

_____

_____

_____

_____

_____

_____

_____

_____

_____

_____

_____

_____

Chapter Nine

Celebrating God Together

s a thoughtful gift is a celebration of a birthday, as a special evening out is a celebration of an anniversary, as a warm eulogy is a celebration of life, as a sexual embrace is a celebration of a marriage—so a worship service is a celebration of God.[36]

We all value those times when the family gathers for such special occasions. Festivities shared with others we love lend a certain significance to life's major happenings and serve to remind us that we belong to someone—that we're part of a family. Behind every successful celebration lies much planning and effort. The same holds true for the corporate celebration of God. Our individual lifestyles of worship culminate in the weekly worship service. "We must understand that getting anything *out* of worship depends directly on our willingness to put effort *in* to it!"[37]

This may mean allowing God to make major changes in personal attitudes, habits, and use of time. That, in itself, challenges us enough, but when we come together in fellowship with other believers we face added difficulties. However great the challenge, it's well worth the effort. In the same way a gardener cultivates the earth before anyone can enjoy the beautiful aroma of a rose, the body of believers undergoes a kind of cultivation process. The flower of worship will come to full bloom and emanate a heavenly fragrance to the Father only after He has prepared the ground.

A lost world cannot help but be drawn to and affected by the true Body of Christ that worships in harmony. Like the early believers in the book of Acts, the Church today would be better able to make an impact.

> *And when they heard this, they lifted their voices to God with one accord and said, "O Lord, it is Thou who didst make the heaven and the earth and the sea, and all that is in them . . ." And when they had prayed, the place where they had gathered together was shaken, and they were all filled with the Holy Spirit, and began to speak the word of God with boldness. And the congregation of those who believed were of one heart and one soul.*
>
> Acts 4:24,31,32a

"Many go to church. Few go to worship," announced a church billboard in Nashville. How accurate! The Christian community practices its beliefs in many ways, but does a desire to worship form the basis for all our activity? In the meetings there may be preaching, confession of sins and assurances of forgiveness, Scripture reading, communion and baptism. The church sanctions marriages, participates in public prayer and sings hymns. We may even be well-known for musical ability, but what motive lies at the core of all these experiences?

Worship *should* be. Adoration of God should be at the center of every aspect of our lives. Activities, functions and ceremonies take place in the name of Jesus and yet, His presence does not permeate them. If the worship we experience does not give us "courage in the night, joy in the dawn" and power for service, then it is only a mere facsimile of the real thing.[38] When we do all in His name to glorify Him, we approach genuine worship.

> Worship is the one religious activity that lends itself to such a delicate blending of different heritages, for worship is so Christ-centered and requires such a God-consciousness that participants must look away from themselves in order to worship.[39]

Unfortunately, more strife occurs because of differences of opinion about worship than perhaps any other area of faith. As Christians, we all agree on certain basic doctrinal truths, but we may have to remind ourselves of the need for individuality in worship. Within the bounds of Scripture, everyone needs the freedom to express his or her own heartfelt love of God. Our way is not the only way. Others may be just as sincere and growing equally as close to the Lord.

No matter what prior church experience we have, we struggle to achieve a scriptural balance in the three major dimensions of love. You may remember from our study of the love triangles in chapter two that *worship* is the motivational factor. It spurs us on to acquire increased *knowledge* and to develop a stronger *covenant* with the Lord.

We noted the types of churches lacking the all-important component of worship. Either a man-made ritualistic formula or a Pharisaical intellectualism characterizes the coldness of these assemblies. As we mentioned earlier also, ritual has some value if worship builds on that firm foundation. Congregational worship for the Old

Testament Jews always began with ritual, proceeded on to worship and finally to the High Priest's oneness with God—one, two, three. Just as a man's bones give support and shape to his body, so too, can meaningful ritual draw people together and lend solidity to worship.

In contrast to cold, dry churches, we learned that an overabundance of worship without an equal measure of the two remaining elements renders a body of believers just as unhealthy. For us to develop a positive, growing love relationship with God, all three components flow together in harmony! Indeed, maintaining this balance seems difficult enough in our personal walk. What happens in an assembly?

During congregational worship, our eyes tend to wander and focus on man rather than on God. If we find ourselves distracted by the way others worship, and if we allow personal prejudice to hinder us, we will be unable to sense God's glory. Those of us who grew up in traditional denominations may tend to shy away from people who lift their hands during prayer and worship. But why? It's only a symbol of releasing everything into God's more-than-capable hands. Besides, if the truth of the matter be known, much scriptural support exists for this practice, while there's no biblical precedent for the folding of hands.

Lift up your hands in the sanctuary, and bless the Lord.
                                                    Psalm 134:2

May my prayer be counted as incense before Thee; the lifting up of my hands as the evening sacrifice.
                                                    Psalm 141:2

Then Solomon stood before the altar of the Lord in the presence of all the assembly of Israel and spread out his hands toward heaven.
                                                    I Kings 8:22

Therefore I want the men in every place to pray, lifting up holy hands, without wrath and dissension.
                                                    I Timothy 2:8

❦

Setting aside preconceived notions and personal inhibitions is certainly not easy, but necessary. Other things also occur during communal worship that bring out our intolerance. However, the Scriptures exhort us throughout not to abandon the idea of getting together,

> *Not forsaking our own assembling together, as is the habit of some, but encouraging one another; and all the more, as you see the day drawing near.*
>
> Hebrews 10:25

In every gathering of New Testament worshippers, we see, first of all, that they were committed followers of Jesus Christ. Christians today, as well as then, come together in the precious name of Jesus—in His honor and by His authority. Then we have a thrilling promise to believe in and proclaim: *"For where two or three have gathered together in My name, **there I am in the midst of them**"* (Matthew 18:20).

When we look to the early church for enlightenment about these gatherings, we see some situations well worth noting. Every assembly governed itself by the Word, and was separated from the others because of distance only. In each locale, all believers came together as one group. Nowhere do we find reference to any such thing as denominations—only believers and unbelievers. In fact, the Apostle Paul reprimanded those who did attempt to separate for one reason or another,

> *"Now I exhort you, brethren, by the name of our Lord Jesus Christ, that you all agree, and there be no divisions among you, but you be made complete in the same mind and in the same judgment. Has Christ been divided? Paul was not crucified for you, was he? Or were you baptized in the name of Paul?"*
>
> I Corinthians 1:10,13

While adoration of God remains the primary purpose for congregational worship, mutual encouragement is another important reason for gathering together. Yet, this time of worship does not take place on a free-for-all basis. The Holy Spirit, if given freedom to move, will still maintain certain principles of order. God doesn't stir up confusion! (I Corinthians 14:33). Paul's epistle to the Ephesian church tells us to rejoice together in the Spirit of God rather than to seek earthly bliss, *"Speaking to one another in psalms and hymns and spiritual songs, singing and making melody with your heart to the Lord . . ."* (Ephesians 5:19).

The only restrictions he placed upon singing, dancing, shouting, weeping and spiritual gifts? Do them to the glory of God and to build up His body, the Church. In the 14th chapter of I Corinthians we see a few guidelines concerning the use of spiritual gifts in a congregation,

> *"What then is the outcome, brethren? When you assemble, each one has a psalm, has a teaching, has a revelation, has a tongue, has an interpretation. Let all things be done for edification. If anyone speaks in a tongue, it should be by two or at the most three, and each in turn, and let one interpret; but if there is no interpreter, let him keep silent in the church; and let him speak to himself and to God. And let two or three prophets speak, and the others pass judgment."*
>
> I Corinthians 14:26-29

In the book of Timothy, Paul encouraged saints to read the Word as an essential part of group worship, *"Until I come, give attention to the public reading of Scripture, to exhortation and teaching"* (I Timothy 4:13). Paul also urged that the various congregations share his letters. This kept the lines of communication open and promoted evenly balanced growth throughout the entire body of Christ (I Thessalonians 5:27, Colossians 4:16).

Yes, all of these activities should take place during a worship service based on biblical principles. If we want to revitalize our love relationship with God, then we must seek to restore worship to its rightful position. Let's look at some scriptural examples of congregational assemblies where the glory and power of God came to dwell—even in the Old Testament before Jesus came in the flesh.

The time was shortly after David, as king of Israel, defeated the Philistine army from Geba to Gazer and brought the ark of God to the city of Jerusalem. The whole nation of Israel turned out for this great event. II Samuel 6 describes the entire account, but we'll concentrate on those verses pertaining to praise and worship,

> *Now David again gathered all the chosen men of Israel, thirty thousand. Meanwhile, David and all the house of Israel were celebrating before the Lord with all kinds of instruments made of fir wood, and with lyres, harps, tambourines, castanets and cymbals. And so it was, that when the bearers of the ark of the Lord had gone six paces, he sacrificed an ox and a fatling. And David was dancing before the Lord with all his might, and David was wearing a linen ephod. So David and all the house of Israel were bringing up the ark of the Lord with shouting and the sound of the trumpet. So they brought in the ark of the Lord and set it in its place inside the tent which David had pitched for it; and David offered burnt offerings and peace offerings before the Lord. And when David had finished offering the burnt offering and the peace offering, he blessed the people in the name of the Lord of hosts.*

II Samuel 6:5,13-15,17,18

Although there was order in everything that took place, freedom and joy flowed in their worship. In spite of the criticism King David's wife voiced for his lack of "propriety," he was committed to worshipping the Lord with all his heart.

Another example of superb congregational worship occurred when Solomon dedicated the newly-completed temple. The

priests had set the ark of the covenant in its position of reverence
in the holy of holies and the following took place,

> And when the priests came forth from the holy place
> (for all the priests who were present had sanctified
> themselves, without regard to divisions), and all the
> Levitical singers, Asaph, Herman, Jeduthun and their
> sons and kinsmen, clothed in fine linen, with cym-
> bals, harps, and lyres, standing east of the altar, and
> with them one hundred twenty priests blowing
> trumpets in unison when the trumpeters and the
> singers were to make themselves heard with one voice
> accompanied by trumpets and cymbals and instru-
> ments of music, and when they praised the Lord
> saying, "He indeed is good for His lovingkindness is
> everlasting," then the house, the house of the Lord,
> was filled with a cloud, so that the priests could not
> stand to minister because of the cloud, **for the glory
> of the Lord filled the house of God."**
>
> II Chronicles 5:11-14

At this point Solomon addressed all of the people and
blessed them as they stood before the Lord. After a brief word
to them, Solomon prayed and. . .*kneeled down upon his knees
before all the congregation of Israel, and spread forth his hands
toward heaven* (II Chronicles 6:13b). David and the people had
fulfilled God's requirements for coming into His presence. Note
God's response and that of the people,

> Now when Solomon had finished praying, fire came
> down from heaven and consumed the burnt offering
> and the sacrifices and the glory of the Lord filled the
> house. And the priests could not enter into the house
> of the Lord, because **the glory of the Lord filled the
> Lord's house**. And all the sons of Israel, seeing the

fire come down and the glory of the Lord upon the house, bowed down on the pavement with their faces to the ground, and they worshipped and gave praise to the Lord, saying, "Truly He is good, truly His loving-kindness is everlasting."

II Chronicles 7:1-3

When the presence of Almighty God descended, the glory was so awesome that the priests could not even enter the temple. Imagine how humbling to all those present! They knew without a doubt that there was a God whose name was Jehovah. Their only response? Worship.

Let's look at one more Old Testament model of genuine communal worship—during the time of the rebuilding of Jerusalem recounted in the book of Nehemiah,

And all the people gathered as one man at the square which was in front of the Water Gate, and they asked Ezra the scribe to bring the book of the law of Moses which the Lord had given to Israel. Then Ezra the priest brought the law before the assembly of men, women, and all who could listen with understanding. . .and he read from it before the square which was in front of the Water Gate from early morning until midday. . .and all the people were attentive to the book of the law. And Ezra blessed the Lord, the great God. And all the people answered, "Amen, Amen!" while lifting up their hands; then they bowed low and worshipped the Lord with their faces to the ground. Also Jeshua. . .and the Levites explained the law to the people while the people remained in their place. And they read from the book, from the law of God, translating to give the sense so that they understood the reading. Then Nehemiah, who was the governor, and Ezra the priest and scribe, and the Levites who taught the people said to all the people,

"This day is holy to the Lord your God; do not mourn or weep." For all the people were weeping when they heard the words of the law.

Nehemiah 8:1,3,5-9

We find here, the reality of John MacArthur's affirmation,

Worship is not an emotional exercise with God-words that induce certain feelings. Worship is a response built upon truth. . . If we are to worship in truth, and the Word of God is truth, we must worship out of an understanding of the Word of God.[40]

In the passage in Nehemiah, we can see the tremendous power of the Scriptures when read and explained to an assembly under the anointing of the Holy Spirit. It convicted them so much, they cried. Oh, that we would have such power behind our teaching today!

We can't mistake the importance of saints gathered together in worship. "What do these examples have to do with us?" we might wonder. Since they occurred in the Old Testament before Jesus, do they apply to us today?

Yes. It's true, we do live under a new covenant with the Father now. No longer do we live bound to a regimen of Jewish law, but we enjoy grace by faith in Jesus. Love and dependence on Him gives us the *ability* to keep His commands and to worship Him fully. As we have stated, the manner in which God deals with us now differs from His treatment of the children of Israel prior to the birth, death and resurrection of Jesus. Yet, neither His principles nor His desire for worship have changed. *Jesus Christ is the same yesterday and today, yes and forever* (Hebrews 13:8).

In his book **Real Worship,** Warren Wiersbe notes that someone asked him this same question. His reply, in part, was as follows,

The Old Testament legal ceremonies were fulfilled in Christ, so we do not repeat them today. But I see no reason why we must make an artificial distinction between "Old Testament worship" and "New Testament worship" when we see no such distinction in Scripture.[41]

From the aforementioned patterns of worship, we can derive an all-important truth. In each case, worship took place in simple response to a manifestation or revelation of the glory of the Lord. Worship burst forth from the hearts of the people like a river overcoming a dam. How much more true should this be for us today, who have the Spirit of God dwelling in our hearts?

A.P. Gibbs rendered the following beautiful description of the source and destination of this powerful river within us. Christ used the analogy of living water to describe the spiritual life which He came to make possible to all who believe,

> *"Everyone who drinks of this water shall thirst again; but whoever drinks of the water that I shall give him shall become in him a well of water springing up to eternal life."*
>
> John 4:13,14

This living water fills the believer at the new birth. It springs up within him in worship. It then flows out from him in service.

> *"If any man is thirsty, let him come to Me and drink. He who believes in Me, as the Scripture said, From his innermost being shall flow rivers of living water."*
>
> John 7:37-39

Long ago Solomon made the observation that even though all the rivers ran into the sea, the sea never became any fuller nor the rivers emptier,

All the rivers flow into the sea, yet the sea is not full.
To the place where the rivers flow, there they flow again.

Ecclesiastes 1:7,8

For the spiritual river to flow freely through us, we have to first release it in worship to its ultimate Source. "The spiritual life which flows from God to us returns to Him in worship from us, and thus the divine cycle is complete."[42]

FIRE-SEEKER'S COMPANION
Questions for Group Interaction
or Individual Reflection

1. What does a worship service have in common with birthday gifts/parties or an evening out with your mate on your anniversary? Does it have that excitement at your church? Why or why not and what can you do?

2. What happened when believers got together in the book of Acts? Can that kind of impact happen again today? Who joins the celebration when Christians worship in unity?

3. What should be the goal of all church activities? Why does worship help bring people of many different backgrounds and personalities together? At the same time, what makes group worship a challenge?

4. Were there denominations in the early church? What separated believers? How were the different groups governed? Besides adoration of God, what should happen when believers worship together?

5. Describe the setting and reason for King David's grand worship service. What took place there? And King Solomon's service—what was it like and why were they celebrating? How about the gathering under Ezra? Compare and contrast it with the other two.

6. What role does the Word of God play in congregational worship? Do Old Testament ceremonies apply to us? Why? What does each celebration we studied have in common with true worship today?

7. Compare a river with a lifestyle of worship. What does that mean to you? Would you describe yourself as exhibiting a trickle, a stream, or a fast-flowing river? What can you do about it?

OPEN SHARING: FEEL FREE TO DISCUSS QUESTIONS OR ANYTHING RELATED TO THE CHAPTER THAT MINISTERED TO MEMBERS OF THE GROUP. LET THE HOLY SPIRIT LEAD YOU.

Fire-starter's Preparation
("Lab" Exercise)

SPEND TIME ALONE AND TOGETHER WORSHIPPING THE LORD. BEFORE AND AFTER, RECORD YOUR THOUGHTS AND FEELINGS IN A JOURNAL. WRITE DOWN CHANGES YOU NOTICE IN YOUR LIFE.

NOTES

_____

_____

_____

_____

_____

_____

_____

_____

_____

_____

_____

_____

_____

_____

_____

_____

_____

_____

_____

_____

Chapter Ten

Obstacles

iants dwell in the land of worship. But, "God names the giants. . . presents His battle strategy and leads on to victory. Worship is worth the warfare."[43] Such dangers have as their source, as quoted by A.P. Gibbs, one or more of the following three things, "the devil, the infernal enemy, the world, the external enemy, and the flesh, the internal enemy."[44] *Anything* will try to climb onto the throne of our hearts where God should reign.

In II Corinthians, Paul classified all mankind into three groups: natural, carnal and spiritual man. The renowned twentieth-century Chinese preacher and teacher of the Word, Watchman Nee, wrote extensively on this subject. In his three-volume series, **The Spiritual Man,** he defined these groups.

Natural man has been separated from God as result of Adam's sin and ensuing fall from grace. *Carnal* or *soulish* man has

❧

been redeemed from eternal death by belief in the blood of Jesus Christ. The Holy Spirit has come to live within him, but the flesh—his body and soul (mind, will or emotions)—rules him. Only the *spiritual* man submits himself completely to the Holy Spirit. His human spirit, led by the Spirit of God, directs his body and soul.

Natural man cannot worship because he has no relationship with God. He is Creator to him, but not Lord. Carnal or soulish man cannot experience true worship because his own humanity tosses him about. The spiritual man alone worships in the beauty of holiness because his spirit communes directly with the Spirit of God. He yields to the Holy Spirit's leading.

God has placed within every born-again believer the desire to worship. But the carnal man, because he does not walk in the Spirit, trips over obstacles and gets ensnared in pitfalls to worship. As Christians, we're *in* the world, but not *of* it. We have the power to say "no" to the selfish things of life and "yes" to God and His commandments. To become true worshippers, we need to maintain that all-important balance in our love relationship with God, and be willing to leave behind every obstacle and pitfall as vanquished foes. There is no other way.

Pride

Pride completely obstructs worship. It stands as our greatest stumbling-block to a wonderful adventure.

Pride is a subtle thing and often exists where it is least expected, for one can even be proud of his humility! Pride in one's own personal appearance leads that individual to give undue attention to himself, or herself. Pride of gift leads to an osten-tatious display of it and a secret craving for applause. Pride of position leads its owner to adopt a conde-scending air to his fellow believers. Pride of posses-sions shows itself in self-complacency and boasting. Pride of one's ecclesiastical position evidences itself in smugness and sanctimoniousness.[45]

❦

Lucifer led worship in heaven. He walked closest to the throne of the Almighty, until he became prideful and wanted to take God's place,

> *"You were the anointed cherub who covers (the throne), and I placed you there. You were on the holy mountain of God; You walked in the midst of the stones of fire. You were blameless in your ways from the day you were created, until unrighteousness was found in you."*
>
> Ezekiel 28:14,15

This very fault of pride led to Lucifer's rebellion against God and to his ruin,

> *"How you have fallen from heaven, O star of the morning, son of the dawn! You have been cut down to the earth, you who have weakened the nations! But you said in your heart, 'I will ascend to heaven; I will raise my throne above the stars of God, and I will sit on the mount of assembly in the recesses of the north. I will ascend above the heights of the clouds; I will make myself like the Most High.'"*
>
> Isaiah 14:12-15

Closely associated with pride is the self-will Lucifer showed when he said, "I will do this," and "I will do that." We see another example of this obstacle in reference to two of the sons of Aaron, the high priest. These men knew the commandments of God regarding proper worship, yet they willfully disobeyed and paid a heavy price,

> Now Nadab and Abihu, the sons of Aaron, took their respective firepans, and after putting fire in them, placed incense on it and offered strange fire before

the Lord, which He had not commanded them. And fire came out from the presence of the Lord and consumed them, and they died before the Lord.

Leviticus 10:1,2

Rebellious pride costs dearly. We have to come to Him on His terms, not ours.

Lack of Knowledge

You may remember from our study of the love triangle that a lack of scriptural knowledge not only keeps us from true worship; we can be easily led astray, sometimes with harmful results. In Hosea, we see that a lack of knowledge serves as a poor excuse for disobedience. As the Scripture says, *"My people are destroyed for lack of knowledge"* (Hosea 4:6).

King David's disastrous first attempt to restore the ark of God to Jerusalem is a prime example. The ark represented the divine presence, the place where He communed with his people through the high priest.

Scriptures plainly taught that only Aaron and his sons could touch the holy things of the tabernacle, while the sons of Kohath were to carry the ark *on poles placed through rings on the top.*

> *And when Aaron and his sons have finished covering the holy objects and all the furnishings of the sanctuary, when the camp is to set out, after that the sons of Kohath shall come to carry them, so they may not touch the holy objects and die. These are the things in the tent of meeting which the sons of Kohath are to carry.*

Numbers 4:15

Since the ark had been missing from the house of Israel for many years, the people may have forgotten the prescribed method for transporting it. What actually took place? I Samuel records the event,

*And they placed the ark of God **on a new cart** so that they might bring it. . .But when they came to the threshing floor of Nacon, Uzzah reached out toward the ark of God and took hold of it, for the oxen nearly upset it. And the anger of the Lord burned against Uzzah, and God struck him down there for his irreverence, and he died there by the ark of God.*

II Samuel 6:6,7

Little did it matter that they tried to use a *new* cart to take the ark to Jerusalem, or that they had good intentions in wanting to restore it there in the first place. Although God does look at our heart in preparation for worship, obedience to His previously stated commands is also important. We can be so thankful for the blood of Jesus, which cleanses us so that our sins might not keep us from the presence of a Holy God.

Independence

We have already used the expressions "dependence" and "interdependence." These develop as our relationship with God deepens. An independent spirit will not long be tolerated in the presence of God. Wanting to be self-reliant and able to suc-ceed on our own skills add up to sin.

As teenagers, we all desired to be "grown-up" and out on our own in the world—independent from both God and fami-ly. During this period in life, many young Christians stray from the Father's embrace and attempt to "do their own thing." Also during this time they make many, sometimes tragic, mistakes as a result of a search for independence.

This is the exact opposite of abiding (making our dwelling) in God and His abiding in us. Jesus said unless we become like children, submissive and dependent, we miss out on His kingdom. Perhaps God tells us to raise our hands in worship as an outward indication of our inner dependency on Him—much like little ones who hold up their hands when they want to be picked up and held by a parent.

Critical Spirit

The habit of finding fault with everything and everyone devastates worship. It runs contrary to the attitudes and actions of Jesus who seeks to deliver us from our sinful ways rather than simply condemn us. When we criticize rather than correct and encourage a brother, we condemn not only him, but ourselves. *Therefore you are without excuse, every man of you who passes judgment, for in that you judge another, you condemn yourself* (Romans 2:1).

Many times we see faults in others that trouble us in ourselves. A critical spirit prevents us from becoming worshippers because it draws our gaze off of the perfection of God and onto the imperfections of mere men, especially *other* men. As long as we're pointing out another's weaknesses, we don't have time to allow God to cleanse us from our own sin. And holiness precedes entering His presence! *Then you will call, and the Lord will answer; You will cry, and He will say, "Here I am." If you remove the yoke from your midst, the **pointing of the finger** . . ."* (Isaiah 58:9).

Laziness

Worship is active, not passive. It demands our all. Laziness should not even come up in the vocabulary of a true worshipper. Instead, he uses words like seek, search, guard, fight, run, plant, sow, reap, build and work . . . work . . . more work. *But prove yourselves to be doers of the word, and not merely hearers who delude themselves* (James 1:22). *Poor is he who works with a negligent hand, but the hand of the diligent makes rich* (Proverbs 10:4).

In Matthew 25, Jesus told the story of a man taking a trip. Before leaving, he entrusted to three servants varying sums of money: five talents, two and one respectively. Two of the servants used what they were given wisely and multiplied it, while the third simply buried his share. Upon the master's return, he rewarded well the two productive servants, while he sent the third one away from his presence,

❦

> *"But his master answered and said to him, 'You wicked, lazy slave, you knew that I reap where I did not sow, and gather where I scattered no seed. . . Therefore take away the talent from him, and give it to the one who has the ten talents. For to everyone who has shall more be given, and he shall have in abundance, but from the one who does not have, even what he does have shall be taken away. And cast out the worthless slave into the outer darkness; in that place there shall be weeping and gnashing of teeth.'"*
>
> Matthew 25:26,28-30

These examples, although given in terms of material wealth, speak also of spiritual treasure. We, as "joint heirs with Jesus," have received much we can use for the glory of God. In order for the spiritual treasure to be multiplied, and for us to be deemed good and faithful servants, we must share what the Lord has given to us. Like the two faithful servants who were diligent in their stewardship, looking expectantly for their master's return, we can do more than simply await the return of our Master and expect to be blessed.

A worshipful life requires much effort and self-sacrifice. The spiritually lazy person is not prepared to enter the presence of God. If we consider worship a duty rather than a passionate response to a loving God, slothfulness can result. When this happens, either individually or collectively, the fires of love grow cold.

Impatience

Failure to wait on God's go-ahead (taking things into our own hands) greatly hinders our relationship with Him. He directs us to *rest in the Lord and wait patiently for Him* (Psalm 37:7); and to *be still and know that He is God* (Psalm 46:10). If we could just learn to say with the psalmist, *My soul, wait in silence for God only, for my hope is from Him* (Psalm 62:5).

Impatience, in direct opposition to God's commands, may lead to even greater sins. Saul, the king of Israel, demonstrated the weakness of impatience while awaiting the return of Samuel, the prophet. The Lord had anointed *Samuel* as a priest whose duty included leading the sacrificial worship before armies left for war. Saul overstepped his bounds and decided to perform the ceremony himself. This one act of disobedience had far-reaching consequences,

> *Now he waited seven days, according to the appointed time set by Samuel, but Samuel did not come to Gilgal; and the people were scattering from him. So Saul said, "Bring to me the burnt offering and the peace offerings." And he offered the burnt offering. And it came about as soon as he finished offering the burnt offering, that behold, Samuel came; and Saul went out to meet him and to greet him. And Samuel said to Saul, "You have acted foolishly; you have not kept the commandment of the Lord your God, which He commanded you, for now the Lord would have established your kingdom over Israel forever. But now your kingdom shall not endure. The Lord has sought out for Himself a man after His own heart. . ."*

I Samuel 13:8,9,13

Saul's failure to wait upon God's man proved disastrous, not only to his worship, but to his future. Likewise for us. Jesus alone has earned the right to be our High Priest who leads us into the presence of God and on to fulfillment in our calling.

Legalism

Do you find yourself doing more and worshipping less? Unable to find time to sing and praise the Lord or to rest in His presence? The need for constant spiritual activity may be associated with the sin of pride. We might be seeking significance through our own works instead of the finished work of Christ. Responsible "Marthas" have their place, but not to the extent that "busy-ness" interferes with an ability to listen, worship and grow in a love of God. Jesus' words to Mary and Martha give us a hint about performance-oriented legalism,

> *And she had a sister called Mary, who moreover was listening to the Lord's word, seated at His feet. But Martha was distracted with all her preparations; and she came up to Him, and said, "Lord, do You not care that my sister has left me to do all the serving alone? Then tell her to help me." But the Lord answered and said to her, "Martha, Martha, you are worried and bothered about so many things; but only a few things are necessary, really only one, for Mary has chosen the good part, which shall not be taken away from her."*
>
> Luke 10:39-42

Emotionalism

Human emotions can hinder the development of a worshipper's heart if they are allowed to rule, unchecked by wisdom. Different emotions affect people in various ways. Unfortunately, the majority have either long or short-range negative consequences. Most of us have had at least a passing acquaintance with anger, anxiety, or depression at one time or another.

During the rebuilding of the wall around Jerusalem, the people reacted emotionally to the enemy's efforts to hinder their project. They became discouraged and unable to work,

> *Thus in Judah it was said, "The strength of the burden bearers is failing, yet there is much rubbish; and we ourselves are unable to rebuild the wall."*
>
> Nehemiah 4:10

Elitism

This phenomenon in the church departs from the truth of the Word. It has wrought havoc in the body of Christ. Wherever the truth—all believers as priests unto the Lord—has been exchanged for the exclusivity of the clergy, it has very nearly destroyed Christians' ability to worship. Bradbent's, **Pilgrim Church,** points out how, by forming a special "caste" called "clergy" (who bear the full responsibility of going before God on behalf of believers), some mainline denominations have departed from the spirit of the New Testament church. Through His victory on the cross, Jesus established the "priesthood of all believers." Any Christian may go boldly before Him to receive grace. This became evident when the veil between the holy and the most holy place was torn in two at the moment of His death.

You also, as living stones, are being built up as a spiritual house for a holy priesthood to offer up spiritual sacrifices acceptable to God through Jesus Christ. . .but you are a chosen race, a royal priesthood, a holy nation, a people for God's own possession, that you may proclaim the excellencies of Him who has called you out of darkness into His marvelous light.

I Peter 2:9

Traditionalism

Many times worship is compromised by theology instead of theology being permeated with worship. Endless questions about non-essentials detract from worship and stifle faith. Formalism, the outward observance of forms, rules, and methods carried to extremes, quenches the Holy Spirit. Do our traditions enhance, rather than hinder, worship? That's the crucial question. Judson Cornwall summed up this idea when he said,

To insist upon doing only what comes naturally is to limit ourselves to the peer pressure and cultural restraints others have place upon us, and this means that we will never rise to a level higher than that which others have chosen for us to attain.[46]

Now the Lord is the Spirit; and where the Spirit of the Lord is, there is liberty (II Corinthians 3:17).

Unforgiveness

Harboring unforgiveness against anyone, whether for real or imagined wrongs, hinders worship. In order to enter God's presence, we must be forgiven and cleansed from all sin,

> *Behold, the Lord's hand is not so short that it cannot save; neither is His ear so dull that it cannot hear. But your iniquities have made a separation between you and your God, and your sins have hidden His face from you, so that He does not hear.*
>
> Isaiah 59:1,2

God won't forgive us if we refuse to forgive others for their offenses. Our Lord makes this clear in the Sermon on the Mount,

> *"And forgive us our debts, as we also have forgiven our debtors. . .for if you forgive men for their trans-gressions, your heavenly Father will also forgive you. But if you do not forgive men, then your heavenly Father will not forgive your transgressions."*
>
> Matthew 6:12,13

Unforgiveness devastates communion with God. Whether in the Old Testament or in the New, the Word states repeatedly that the only way to come into His presence is with a heart free from sin. Until we choose to forgive *everyone* of *every* wrong against us, worship will be impossible.

Worldly Influence

The fires of worship will never burn in a heart tainted with an affection for worldliness. The reason for this is simple: no man can serve two masters. He will love one and hate the other. Once we have been born again by the Spirit of the Lord, in essence we no longer belong to this world. We become strangers passing through a foreign land en route to an eternal, heavenly kingdom. When we know this fact, we'll find it easier to say "no" to the world's temporary attractions. Yet, its influence can creep into our lives insidiously if we close our eyes to its dangers. For this reason Jesus prayed,

> *"I do not ask Thee to take them out of the world, but to keep them from the evil one. They are not of the world, even as I am not of the world."*
>
> John 17:15,16

> *Do not love the world, nor the things in the world. If anyone loves the world, the love of the Father is not in him. For all that is in the world, the lust of the flesh and the lust of the eyes and the boastful pride of life, is not from the Father, but is from the world.*
>
> I John 2:15,16

Because of the strong magnetic pull of our "flesh," the Bible advises us to not even fellowship with those involved in lusty pursuits. Although we're called to love and minister to them so they might know Christ too, we must remain free from their habits. That's a hard balancing act. Concerning this dangerous influence, we see one more admonition from the Apostle Paul,

> *Do not be bound together with unbelievers; for what partnership have righteousness and lawlessness, or what fellowship has light with darkness? "Therefore, come out from their midst and be separate, says the Lord. . ."*
>
> II Corinthians 6:14,17

This separation involves more than just an outward physical separation. How about the realm of thought life? We can sit in church and, from all outward appearances, be gloriously worshipping the Lord. Meanwhile our mind stays preoccupied with the cares of life. But we can't fantasize about an affair or think about the latest sale at the mall and worship. God deserves our undivided attention.

Consider Lot's wife and the influence the perverse city of Sodom held over her. When an angel commanded the family to leave Sodom before the Lord would destroy it by fire, *she looked back.* She was destroyed along with the rest of the city. Though attractively camouflaged, Satan uses the things of the world for one ultimate goal—to cause us to spend eternity separated from God. If we forego fellowship with darkness, we'll be able to have sweet communion with Him who is Light.

FIRE-SEEKER'S COMPANION
Questions for Group Interaction or Individual Reflection

1. The Apostle Paul and Watchman Nee "classified" people into three spiritual categories which line up with the Word. What are they? Describe the differences and how they affect worship. How would you rate yourself?

2. Give some examples of pride. What does pride have to do with Satan (formerly Lucifer) and worship? With you?

3. How did Nadab and Abihu sin and what were the consequences? What happened to Uzzah and why? How do these stories apply to you?

4. How does independence affect worship? A critical spirit? Laziness? Why did Saul's impatience get him in trouble? Do these same ones hinder you?

5. How did legalism make Martha behave? Contrast her with Mary. What hindered the rebuilding of the wall in Jerusalem? Does the same happen to you as you try to do something "as unto the Lord"?

6. Elitism—give an example and explain its negative influence on freedom of worship. How about traditionalism?

7. What is the danger of unforgiveness in relation to worship? Can you pray for those *who spitefully use you?* Worldliness keeps us from worshipping God. Why? What happened to Lot's wife?

OPEN SHARING: FEEL FREE TO DISCUSS QUESTIONS OR ANYTHING RELATED TO THE CHAPTER THAT MINISTERED TO MEMBERS OF THE GROUP. LET THE HOLY SPIRIT LEAD YOU.

FIRE-STARTER'S PREPARATION
("Lab" Exercise)

SPEND TIME ALONE AND TOGETHER WORSHIPPING THE LORD.
BEFORE AND AFTER, RECORD YOUR THOUGHTS AND FEELINGS IN A
JOURNAL. WRITE DOWN CHANGES YOU NOTICE IN YOUR LIFE.

NOTES

_____

_____

_____

_____

_____

_____

_____

_____

_____

_____

_____

_____

_____

_____

_____

_____

_____

_____

_____

_____

Chapter Eleven

Pitfalls

ore dangers lurk on the path to worship. Most have inherent positive value, but they can easily turn into idols—inappropriate objects of worship. When *anything* receives higher priority than God, we might as well fall into a dark pit. We lose sight of our first love! The foremost commandments reflect His feelings about this issue,

Hear, O Israel! The Lord is our God, the Lord is one! And you shall love the Lord your God with all your heart and with all your soul and with all your might.

Deuteronomy 6:4,5

"Thou shalt have no other gods before me."

Exodus 20:3

❦

We may need to take a close look at priorities and bring them back into perspective. To protect ourselves against idolatry, it helps to recognize who hides behind the scenes trying to steal what rightfully belongs only to God. Satan wants to replace God as the lord of our heart and make us bow in obeisance to him. The devil even tempted Jesus at the beginning of His earthly ministry,

> *Again, the devil took Him to a very high mountain, and showed Him all the kingdoms of the world, and their glory; and he said to Him, "All these things will I give You, if You fall down and worship me."*
>
> Matthew 4:8,9

We have already observed, from reading of Lucifer's fall from heaven, that pride caused his demise. In this conversation with Jesus he was up to his old tactics. Try to get the Lord to worship him? Yes. And we can believe he tries the same with us today.

Most of us think of idols as something we can touch with our hands, such as the false gods or statues of pagan religions. Idolatry is much more common than that. Pagans do bow down to idols, yet more often, modern idolatry takes on a far subtler form in the heart rather than the hands. Satan's attempts to steal our worship of the one true God are extremely deceptive and rarely take the form of a direct frontal attack. Instead, he prefers to sneak in the side door, catching us unaware. To help expose his strategy, we will look at some of our most vulnerable areas.

Self

As far as worship goes, we're our own worst enemy. Our society, especially in America, promotes a philosophy of immediate self-gratification as one of the highest standards of living. Magazines with titles that encourage exaltation of self sell on nearly every magazine rack.

Self-centeredness runs rampant today. Everywhere people in love with themselves boast about their abilities and accomplishments and give no credit to God. Instead, we hear of self-improvement courses, self-esteem, self-will, self, self, self! I heard a saying once, "The trouble with a self-made man is he worships his creator." If we ever want to become worshippers of the living God, we'll have to pull this demonic philosophy out of our lives by the roots. It's called *humanism.*

In 1933, the Humanist Manifesto suggested that the universe was self-existent, not created. It declared war against any belief in the supernatural and the unique religious emotions and attitudes that go hand in hand with that belief. The humanists denied the spiritual foundation upon which our forefathers built this nation. Man alone was responsible for the realization of his dreams—the master of his fate. Contained within man, himself, resided the power for all great achievement, they said. They even felt bold enough to state that God was dead. How contrary to the Scriptures which say, *It is better to trust in the Lord than to put confidence in man* (Psalm 118:8).

We can never be humble enough before God to worship Him if our own personal desires rule. Notice again the tactic Satan uses. In his temptation of Eve, he attacked her in the area of her self-centered wants,

> *When the woman saw that the tree was good for food, and that it was a delight to the eyes, and that the tree was desirable to make one wise, she took from its fruit and ate; and she gave also to her husband with her, and he ate.*

> Genesis 3:6

Unless we want to succumb to the same subtle temptations, we must deny ourselves, take up our cross and follow the Lord with all our heart. That may be easier said than done, but not if we consider the extent to which Jesus denied Himself for us. With every fiber of His being crying for life, He submitted to His Father's will and died so that *we* might live.

Family

The Bible says a great deal about the family relationship. Marriage symbolizes the union between Jesus and His Bride, the Church. Thus, He expects husbands to love their wives the way He loves the Church, and wives to revere their husbands the way the Church reverences Him. In turn, as parents they train their children according to scriptural principles of love and discipline.

Any time a family fails to follow God's divine order (as when the husband allows the wife to "rule the roost," or when children's demands override God's commands—idolatry), confusion and strife ensue. Eli, a priest of Israel, lost the right to lead worship because he had allowed his sons to control him and rebel against God. They did whatever they pleased. The Lord told the prophet Samuel in a vision,

> *"In that day I will carry out against Eli all that I have spoken concerning his house, from beginning to end. For I have told him that I am about to judge his house forever for the iniquity which he knew, because his sons brought a curse on themselves and he did not rebuke them. And therefore I have sworn to the house of Eli that the iniquity of Eli's house shall not be atoned for by sacrifice or offering forever."*
>
> I Samuel 3:12-14

Possessions

Things we own—homes, cars, clothes, or conveniences—may become idols in a hurry. The key to prevent this? Realize we're only temporary stewards of any possessions and not the true owners. Our Father in heaven owns everything. He just lets us use some of it for awhile. In Matthew 6:19-21, Jesus taught the value of maintaining the proper priority regarding possessions,

> *"Do not lay up for yourselves treasures upon earth, where moth and rust destroy, and where thieves break in and steal. But lay up for yourselves treasures in*

heaven, where neither moth nor rust destroys, and
where thieves do not break in or steal; for where your
treasure is, there will your heart be also."

Believers in the book of Acts realized this fact and conducted
their lives accordingly. They shared with one another, not out of
coercion as in communism, but out of love,

And the congregation of those who believed were of
one heart and soul; and not one of them claimed that
anything belonging to him was his own; but all things
were common property to them . . . for there was not a
needy person among them, for all who were owners of
land or houses would sell them and bring the proceeds
of the sales.

Acts 4:32,34

During those days, the greatest revival of worship in history
took place. Signs and wonders were prevalent and everyone spoke
the Word of God with boldness. It must have been a glorious time
when the Holy Spirit moved so mightily among men!

Power

"Power corrupts, and absolute power corrupts absolutely,"
stated a wise man. This expression holds true for today's church
as much as for those involved in the world's system. Believers are
just parts of the body of Christ. He alone is the all-powerful Head.
Even in the early church some people hungered for control over
others. Diotrephes sought a prominent position, as Paul pointed
out, *"I wrote something to the church; but Diotrephes, who loves*
to be first among them, does not accept what we say" (3 John 9).
Compare this to Jesus' answer to a mother's request for her
sons' promotion to the top spot,

"You know that the rulers of the Gentiles lord it over them, and their great men exercise authority over them. It is not so among you, but whoever wishes to become great among you shall be your servant, and whoever wishes to be first among you shall be your slave; just as the Son of Man did not come to be served, but to serve, and to give His life a ransom for many."

Matthew 20:25-28

We have to continually examine and re-examine our motives to insure that we desire to serve rather than be in a position of power. God alone has the title of "boss." We, like Paul, are His bond servants (slaves by choice) if we want to be worshippers after His own heart.

Money

Money—the big scoreboard—is often worshipped in today's society. People study the stock market with zeal, but can't find a moment to study the Word of Life. How many of us have looked to Wall Street for security rather than to Jesus Christ? Money itself doesn't cause problems, but the love of it does (I Timothy 6:10).

Think of the tragic story of Ananias and Sapphira in the book of Acts. During the time when the power of the Holy Spirit was so mighty, people willingly sold their land and possessions in order to give the money to the Lord's work. No one among them lacked anything because of their obedience. Ananias and Sapphira were obedient in selling their property, but they stumbled when the time came to part with the money,

But Peter said, "Ananias, why has Satan filled your heart to lie to the Holy Spirit, and to keep back some of the price of the land?. . . Why is it that you have conceived this deed in your heart? You have not lied to men, but to God." And as he heard these words, Ananias fell down and breathed his last. . .

Acts 5:3,4b,5

Sapphira's love of money caused her to follow in the steps of her husband and suffer the same fatal consequences. Money as an idol leads us all far from God. That doesn't have to happen. We can steer clear of the danger associated with the *love* of money if we devote a good part of our treasure to the God we worship. So spread the Good News!

Occupation

Before we have experienced the joy of true worship, some of us find the business world much more invigorating. America encourages this. Professional success becomes a god of this world. People often feel condemned if they don't spend fifteen hours a day at the office and several more at home with paperwork. "God's Word recognizes the necessity for the Christian to be in business, but warns against business being in the Christian."[47]

The Apostle Paul, a tentmaker by trade (Acts 18:3), used his job as a means of helping to support his ministry. Paul did not order his ministry around his job and neither should we. Whether in full-time Christian service or not, we can still be good stewards who see an occupation as a "platform" to enhance *God's* business—the preaching of the gospel far and near.

Recreation

God has planned for us to enjoy the fruit of our labor. But when the enjoyment of this fruit becomes the sole purpose for laboring, idolatry, like a weed, has taken root. He is not a merciless taskmaster who requires constant work. However, recreation may compete for quality time with Him. When athletics (in itself inherently beneficial), prevents us from reading the Bible or from praying and worshipping God, we'd better regroup.

How much time and money do Americans spend in search of that elusive quality, pleasure? So much recreation offered by the world today bears no resemblance to Scripture, and it concerns me. I'm apprehensive about the effects it will have on my children and future grandchildren because I know that even the best counterfeit is but a poor substitute for time with the Lord. Our choices can help us glorify God and still allow us to worship.

Paul, in his illustrations of the Christian life, made references to a runner in a race as well as a skilled boxer. He gave us the key to balance,

> *For bodily discipline is only of little profit, but godliness is profitable for all things, since it holds promise for the present life and also for the life to come.*
>
> I Timothy 4:8

Recreation and good physical health can enhance our ability to worship. But replace it? Never.

Science

In today's world of expanding technology, science has become an idol—the one used most often to refute the truth of the Bible. When man's learning divorces itself from the knowledge of God, it usually opposes divine revelation found in the Scriptures. If we choose to place our faith in science above the truth of God's Word. . .idolatry again.

Have you heard about the conflict taking place in our nation's schools? It concerns teaching the theory of evolution versus the biblical account of creation. Evolution often gets "better press;" creationism comes out as "myth." Much of this debate rages around the seeming discrepancy between the age of the earth and the length of man's existence on the planet. Yet, a closer look reveals the total awesomeness of our God and declares the absolute truth of His Word. Let's pursue this point a bit further in support of our glorious Lord.

As we first open our Bibles, we see in Genesis 1:1 that, *In the beginning God created the heavens and the earth.* The ultimate beginning of creation! Prior to this in the dateless past, God alone existed. When He created heaven and earth, He included all the stars, the sun and moon, the earth and all the heavenly host: angels, cherubim, seraphim and even that anointed cherub himself, Lucifer.

In the fourteenth chapter of Isaiah, and in the twenty-eighth chapter of Ezekiel, we read about the fall of Lucifer and learned that he was cast from heaven into the earth, *How you have fallen from heaven, O star of the morning, son of the dawn! You have been cut down to the earth. . .* (Isaiah 14:12).

The Bible gives no record of exactly when this event took place. But we do know in Genesis 3 that Satan, disguised as a serpent, tempted Eve in the Garden of Eden. That means Lucifer had already lost his anointed position in heaven by that time.

A careful study of Scripture points to Lucifer's fall having occurred some time after the original creation in Genesis 1:1, and before the condition of the earth as found in Genesis 1:2, *And the earth was formless and void, and darkness was over the surface of the deep; and the Spirit of God was moving over the surface of the waters.* How many years, perhaps millions, took place between these verses, and what occurred, we don't know.

Centuries after Adam and Eve, the prophet Jeremiah saw a vision of the earth in the same condition that Genesis 1:2 describes. He recorded that vision and the causes which led up to a cataclysmic annihilation of life on the entire planet,

> *I looked on the earth, and behold, it was formless and void; and to the heavens, and they had no light. I looked on the mountains, and behold, they were quaking, and all the hills moved to and fro. I looked, and, behold, there was no man, and all the birds of the heavens had fled. I looked, and behold, the fruitful land was a wilderness, and all its cities were pulled down before the Lord, before His fierce anger. For thus says the Lord, "The whole land shall be a desolation, yet I will not execute a complete destruction.*

*For this the earth shall mourn, and the heavens above
be dark, because I have spoken, I have purposed, and
I will not change My mind, nor will I turn from it."*

Jeremiah 4:23-28

This desolation resulted from the Lord's fierce anger, but why was He angry? At some point during the vast time span between the original creation and the destruction, God threw Lucifer down to earth, along with one third of all the angels. Lucifer had so perverted God's creation that He had to destroy it. Consider the description of the earth as found in Genesis 1:2 and the one in Jeremiah's prophetic vision. They're nearly identical.

True to His Word, God did not make a full end of the earth, but began again, as Genesis 1:3 indicates. Maybe what science calls the "big bang theory" refers to the moment God, the Creator, said, *"Let there be light. . ."*

One final point of interest we can't ignore. After God created Adam and Eve He gave them a specific command to *be fruitful and multiply, and **replenish** the earth. . .* (Genesis 1:22). How could they replenish the earth unless it had once before been filled? We need not be deceived by the lies and tricks of the devil. He will go to any lengths to cause us to doubt the authenticity of God's Word, to subvert His authority and ultimately, to destroy our worship of Him.

A. W. Tozer had a straightforward view of lofty matters,

Science of course deals with the relation of things and their effect upon each other. But the plain people, the people who would rather believe than to know, and who would rather worship than to discover—they have a simpler and more beautiful view of the world.[48]

Occult

Millions of Americans saw a movie that came out in the early seventies called, "The Exorcist." It focused on a case of demon possession. However representative of Satan's work as the movie may have been, the devil usually poses in much more subtle and attractive ways. An article about modern-day witches that presented a disguised view appeared in "Insight: The Washington Times."

The article put forth some very disturbing misconceptions that tried to separate the occult practice of witchcraft from Satan. It was effective. Check out the following quotes from letters received in response to the article,

> Avoiding the false Hollywood stereotypes and correctly disassociating both witches and their religion from satanism, the article presented a view of their religion that is believable...

> Witchcraft is flourishing because of its positive benefits to its participants and the entire planet. Most rituals have some focus on healing our ravaged Mother Earth. Women especially are drawn to it because of the emphasis on a female divinity which has been denied us in all Western religions. I find it appalling that satanism is mentioned in the glossary of witchcraft terms. Satan has nothing to do with witchcraft, wicca or paganism. None of these groups even believe in the devil's existence. Most feel that Satan is a figment of the medieval church's collective imagination used to coerce people into becoming tithe-giving churchgoers.

We should make no mistake about these things. Behind all forms of the occult, whether under the guise of religion or not, lies the devil himself. The Word of God is quite clear about who we worship, and equally clear as to what occultish practices we should avoid,

> *There shall not be found among you anyone who makes his son or his daughter pass through the fire, one who uses divination, one who practices witch-*

craft, or one who interprets omens, or a sorcerer, or
one who casts a spell, or a medium or a spiritist, or
one who calls up the dead. For whoever does these
things is detestable to the Lord; and because of these
detestable things the Lord your God will drive them
out before you.

Deuteronomy 18:12-14

This passage covers many activities that may go unrecognized, and may be accepted as "harmless." Even something as seemingly innocent as reading the daily horoscope is risky business. In addition to astrology, the Bible includes warnings against palm reading, fortune-telling, ouija boards, and seances (speaking to departed spirits).

The father of lies himself orchestrates such practices behind the scenes and the Lord forbids all of it—including of course, blatant Satan worship. Sin of this nature affronts the omnipotence and guidance of God. The Old Testament punishment for these practices was severe, *He who sacrifices to any god, other than to the Lord alone, shall be utterly destroyed* (Exodus 22:20).

Although we no longer live under the law, God's principles remain the same. He has not lowered His standards just because we now live under the dispensation of grace. If we want to become worshippers of the living God, we can't leave open doors through which Satan may gain an entrance. An idol doesn't become an idol overnight. It takes time. What may have seemed an innocent activity or a fun game at first leads to bondage. The Holy Spirit of truth will alert us to every dangerous practice if we listen. One author gives a few good guidelines,

> . . . one of the obvious contrasts between response
> to the demonic and response to the Divine is that the
> demonic prefers a mindlessness or trance, but God
> always demands an active mind and will. Relationship
> with God in worship is for the entire person—spirit,
> soul and body—and we are invited to be willing and
> active participants in that experience.[49]

Fire-Seeker's Companion
Questions for Group Interaction
or Individual Reflection

1. What is the foremost commandment? Why? Is God on a super ego-trip? Explain idolatry. Does it happen in America? Who is behind it and why?

2. Self interferes with worship. Why? Define humanism and its dangers. How can family become a pitfall to worship? What happened to Eli?

3. How should we regard possessions? What did believers do in the book of Acts and why? How can a love of power or position inhibit worship? What did Jesus tell a status-conscious mother?

4. Is money a sin? What happened to Ananias and Sapphira and why? Can something as necessary as occupation get in the way of communion with God? How can we avoid that? Is recreation evil?

5. Science hinders worship for many people. Why? What can we do about it? What battle rages in our schools?

6. Name some occultish practices that God forbids. Why is He so adamant about this subject?

7. Think seriously about which obstacles and pitfalls trip *you* up most often. What can you do?

Open Sharing: Feel free to discuss questions or anything related to the chapter that ministered to members of the group. Let the Holy Spirit lead you.

Fire-Starter's Preparation
("Lab" Exercise)

Spend time alone and together worshipping the Lord.
Before and after, record your thoughts and feelings in a
journal. Write down changes you notice in your life.

NOTES

_____

_____

_____

_____

_____

_____

_____

_____

_____

_____

_____

_____

_____

_____

_____

_____

_____

_____

_____

Chapter Twelve

Forever Transformed

*Christian worship is the most **momentous**, the most **urgent**, the most **glorious** action that can take place in human life.*
                                        Karl Barth

ORSHIP!
Momentous—significant. . .decisive. . .pivotal.
Urgent—compelling. . .imperative. . .crucial.
Glorious—superb. . .transcendent. . .sublime.
And the *superlative* of all these adjectives describes worship. Does it hold such an esteemed position in your life? For a Christian, worship should form the hub around which the wheel of life revolves. His or her time ceases to be controlled by the routine of living. A worshipper has renounced the habit of just going through the motions in the first few moments of Sunday morning church service. It's easy to do "outward spiritual calisthenics," as Bob Mumford puts it, without the heart even getting warmed up.

As you well know, total transformation does not happen over-night. Or without struggle. But no one who has entered the presence of Almighty God has ever left untouched by His hand.

In holy intimacy, the true worshipper comes face to
face with God and he is transformed by the glory. If
the corporate worship in the church leaves people
unchanged, the church is not really worshipping. If
what goes on in a church service does not spur the
saints to greater obedience, call it what you will, it
isn't worship. Worship always results in a transformation and the church is edified by it.[50]

Moses' experience at the burning bush forever changed
him and left him with a new purpose in life. The prophet Isaiah,
another man who looked up to see the glory of God, was
changed. He became the most well-known Old Testament
prophet because of the revelation God gave him of the coming
Messiah. Ezekiel saw God's glory and became the prophet and
watchman of Israel. Each transformation occurred after a vision
of the glory of the Lord. The same holds true for us today.

After we finally acknowledge that God alone can satisfy
the hunger within, and we set our hearts to become worshippers,
the process of change begins. He smooths some of the rough
edges that prevent us from enjoying Him. Then one day while
our spirits are gazing up, we too, catch a glimpse of the glory
of the Lord. Seeing the "utter and awesome holiness of God,"
and "ourselves against the backdrop of that holiness," our lives
cannot help but be forever changed.[51]

You may remember from the triangles in Part One that
worship is the *motivational* aspect of a relationship with God.
It keeps the fires of the heart burning brightly, regardless of
situations in which we find ourselves. Worship lifts the spirit to
soar heavenward. Although our lives may be filled with physical
suffering, we can still rejoice. Passionate, fiery *worship,* when
balanced with a well-founded *knowledge* and steadfast *covenant*
with the Lord, makes the following promise a reality: *But in all
these things we overwhelmingly conquer through Him who
loved us* (Romans 8:37).

The Apostle Paul provides a prime example of such an overcomer who underwent a radical change. With the misguided zeal of a legalistic Pharisee, Saul (his name before conversion) sought authorization from the highest Jewish officials to persecute believers. One day he had an experience on the road to Damascus that blinded him for three days (Acts 9:3-6). It changed him *spiritually* forever. He met the resurrected Jesus! Three days of darkness marked the beginning of a lifetime of enlightened worship for Paul. From then on, even amidst the harshest circumstances possible, he maintained profound inner joy and wrote a large portion of the New Testament. Paul could write with confidence because he had learned the truth for himself.

> . . . *in far more labors, in far more imprisonments, beaten times without number, often in danger of death. Five times I received from the Jews thirty-nine lashes, three times I was beaten with rods, once I was stoned, three times I was shipwrecked, a night and a day I have spent in the deep. I have been on frequent journeys, in dangers from rivers, dangers from robbers, dangers from my countrymen, dangers from the Gentiles, dangers in the city, dangers in the wilderness, dangers on the sea, dangers among false brethren; I have been in labor and hardship, through many sleepless nights, in hunger and thirst, often without food, in cold and exposure. . .*

II Corinthians 11:23b-27

Amazing, isn't it, that throughout all his tribulations Paul continued to say, *Rejoice evermore* (I Thessalonians 5:16). Whether his walk with the Lord led him over mountains or through valleys, Paul's ability to worship remained steadfast. He produced rich, abundant fruit wherever he went.

As our personal lives of worship progress from glory to glory. . .as we discover what it really means to *abide* in God's presence, the Holy Spirit will bring forth fruit in us, too. We mentioned them earlier, *love, joy, peace, long-suffering, gentleness, goodness, faith, meekness, temperance*... (Galatians 5:22,23).

Note the condition Jesus placed on our ability to bear fruit,

> *"I am the vine, you are the branches; he who abides in Me, and I in him, he bears much fruit; for* **apart from Me you can do nothing**. . .*If you abide in Me, and My words abide in you, ask whatever you wish, and it shall be done for you. By this is My Father glorified, that you bear much fruit, and prove to be My disciples."*
>
> John 15:5,7,8

The transformation in us also resembles the process by which a plain stone, in the hands of a master sculptor, becomes a work of art. Michelangelo once described his talent as an ability to see the masterpiece hidden within the block of marble and then to release it. God sees a saint contained within our rough exteriors. As we abide in Jesus and worship Him, the Holy Spirit brings forth another "masterpiece" for His glory.

Coupled with this freedom to worship comes a greater responsibility and renewed call to holiness. Only *after* God commanded Moses to build a tabernacle, the "pattern" for all true worship, did He say, *"You shall be holy, for I the Lord your God am holy"* (Leviticus 19:2). The Lord knew that neither the Israelites nor we could even begin to fulfil this command until we would learn to worship.

As God leads us toward holiness we will fail, but He can still use periods of reversal to develop character. *If* we view them from the proper perspective. *If* we endure with patience. *If* we continue to rise above failures and rejoice in our total dependency upon Him. Then our lives will become a pleasing fragrance to Him.

Erwin Lutzer, author of **Failure—The Back Door to Success,** emphasizes the advantages of occasional setbacks. We needn't grow frustrated or discouraged because of newly-discovered shortcomings. Rather, we can take heart in God's faithfulness and draw near to Him. In His presence is *fullness of joy* and in His *right hand there are pleasures forevermore!* (Psalm 16:11).

> The fuel of worship is a true vision of the greatness of God; the fire that makes the fuel burn white-hot is the quickening of the Holy Spirit; the furnace made alive and warm by the flame of truth is our renewed spirit; the resulting heat of our affections is powerful worship, pushing its way out in confessions, longings, acclamations, tears, songs, shouts, bowed heads, lifted hands and obedient lives.[52]

Yes, worship accomplishes great things for God, both in and through the believer, but we fight a tremendous battle to do it. Why? Why has Satan gone to such great lengths to distort the truth of this glorious encounter and distract us from it? Why has he tried to make believers apprehensive about coming into the presence of Almighty God? Simple. He knows the power of worship. Do you remember? Before Lucifer (Satan's former name) fell from heaven, he had a very important job as the anointed cherub. He led worship of the Father.

When the body of Christ begins to worship God as He intends, we will experience the greatest move of the Holy Spirit this world has ever imagined. Satan will do everything he can to prevent such a spiritual explosion, but his plans are doomed. The Word promises that when the Bridegroom returns to receive His Bride, the Church, she will be spotless! Through perfect love—*worship,* based on *knowledge,* leading to *covenant*—God will accomplish this feat in us.

Let's do an honest self-evaluation. How appreciative are we of God's "unspeakable gift"? Do we, like the canines Monarch and Mitzi, *respond* to our Master? With open gratitude? Exuberant anticipation? Eagerness to please Him? Can others see, from looking at our day-to-day lives, that an all-consuming love for God motivates us? Do we burn like lights in a darkened world? Worshippers not only burn, they glow.

Worship involves giving something back to God. In a spirit of thankfulness, we present Him a gift for who He is and what He has done because *The Lord has done great things for us; we are glad* (Psalm 126:3). Some people wonder what they can give the Lord that He doesn't already have. He owns the earth in all its fullness. What more is left? The best thing we can give Him is what He gave us: our lives. Our free will. Out of love, we can submit them to Him.

Just as the Hebrew priests offered sacrifices in the tabernacle. . .and Jesus offered Himself as the ultimate sacrifice on the cross, we relinquish any "rights" we think we have to ourselves. What does the God of the whole universe want with us? He wants us to be washed in the blood of the Lamb, filled with His Spirit and consecrated to serve Him.

Paul wrote in Romans that this kind of sacrifice leads not to physical death as it did for Jesus, but to a brand new life—one of service,

> *I urge you therefore, brethren, by the mercies of God, to present your bodies a living and holy sacrifice, acceptable to God, which is your* **spiritual service of worship***.*

> Romans 12:1

Although He does want us to soar in worship's abandon, we must still come down to earth. In other words, not wind up "so heavenly minded that we're of no earthly good." Mountain-tops of praise and worship enable us to return to the valleys and *be loving servants!*

Ronald Allen and Gordon Borror noted the close tie between worship and service,

> How are we fully to love one another as Christ loved us if we do not practice loving God? How can we possibly love lost mankind except to see them as God sees them? We cannot see from His point of view until we know Him.[53]

As we allow the Lord to develop within us the heart attitudes of a true servant, we become more like Jesus. He said,

> *". . .whoever wishes to become great among you shall be your servant; and whoever wishes to be first among you shall be slave of all. For even the Son of Man did not come to be served, but to serve, and to give His life a ransom for many."*
>
> Mark 10:43-45

Effective Christian service flows from a heart that acknowledges the glory, majesty and power of One who is *King,* yet who came to *serve.* As we understand this and learn to love Him deeply, we won't have to "drum up" motivation. Dead obedience will fall by the wayside. Rather, our spirits will radiate the joy of salvation in all our work. The king of servanthood will empower us to worship in everything we do, which in turn, leads to a greater desire to continue serving. Then, *the joy of the Lord is our strength* (Nehemiah 8:10).

When we ripen into such spiritual maturity, we experience new freedom. In a sense, something cushions us from the anxieties of the world. No longer do fear and frustration keep us chained to distorted views of Christian service. Cold, ritualistic religion with its infamous "good deed-doing" melts under a heart aflame. Fiery worship gives birth to genuine service that springs out of a purified heart.

Service never *replaces* worship; rather, service *results* from worship. There lies the key to reaching out to others with an attitude of gratitude. Worship first, serve second. The divine order is important. We see this same association in the words of Jesus during His temptation in the wilderness, *"Begone, Satan! For it is written, 'You shall **worship** the Lord your God, and **serve** Him only'"* (Matthew 4:10).

As we have seen, worship is a spontaneous and dynamic expression of heartfelt emotion—a response on our part to God's greatness. Or as someone said, "Worship is the occupation of the heart, not with its needs or even with its blessings, but with God, Himself." That means referring to ourselves with modesty, as King David did after he learned what great things were in store for him.

> *For Thou knowest Thy servant, O Lord God! For the sake of Thy word, and according to Thine own heart, Thou hast done all this greatness to let Thy servant know. For this reason Thou art great, O Lord God; for there is none like Thee, and there is no God besides Thee...*
>
> II Samuel 7:20-22

Can we rest in God's presence long enough to let Him create pure hearts in us? Any other form of service turns out to be a cheap imitation. It fades away. By comparison, "The work done by a worshipper will have eternity in it."[54]

A word of caution: we can get pretty adept at counterfeit ministry. In order to further our own selfish ambitions, we can even fool ourselves. Our efforts to serve God lead us to put up a facade, a kind of whitewashed fence for others to see. We slip on an attractive covering to camouflage our old, hateful selves. No inner change of heart occurs daily. We lack sincerity, one could say. A brief study of the word *sincere* will give us a better understanding of counterfeit service.

Sincerity is related to a phrase "sin cero," meaning "without wax." In ancient Greece, when a master sculptor completed a flawless piece of art, he had no need to cover it with wax to give a smooth appearance. Less skilled sculptors melted wax to hide the cracks and chips in the "untrue" marble. The most reputable craftsmen marked their expensive creations, "sin cero." Could God hang a "sin cero" tag on us?

We gain sincerity through communion with Him. In His holy presence, He exposes the false and sanctifies us through repentance. He alone can keep us from becoming polished apples with rotten cores! Genuine fruit of the Spirit—*love, joy, peace, long-suffering, gentleness, meekness and temperance*—grow only in the rich environment of the Cross.

God the Father has given every believer all he or she will ever need to serve Him—that is, when we come to Him in our weakness. We don't have to work for Him in our own strength. We needn't depend on our own abilities. How, then, can we accomplish what He gives us to do? In the book of Zechariah we find God's answer, which is just as true for us today, . . . *This is the word of the Lord to Zerubbabel saying, "Not by might nor by power, but by my Spirit," says the Lord of hosts* (Zechariah 4:6).

Ministry, then, is accomplished through the anointing of the Holy Spirit. As our worship experience with the Spirit develops, our capacity for service expands. We become extensions of His love. His gifts pass through our hands to the surrounding world, effecting changes in it. "Truly, those who worship most will serve God best, and only the Spirit can supply the power for both."[55]

God the Father wants His children to continue the task of saving the world! He does it by building up His Church through the anointing and gifts of the Holy Spirit. The Church has one head—Jesus,

> *He also is head of the body, the church, and He is the beginning, the first-born from the dead; so that He Himself might come to have first place in everything.*
>
> Colossians 1:18

For the shepherding and perfecting of His body, Jesus established certain governmental offices, commonly referred to as the "five-fold ministry." Paul enumerated them in his letter to the Ephesian church: the apostle, prophet, evangelist, pastor and teacher. Not everyone is called to be the pastor of a church or an international evangelist like Billy Graham. Yet, God summons each of us to serve and has given us at least one supernatural gift to compensate for our weakness,

> *Now there are **varieties of gifts,** but **the same Spirit.** And there are **varieties of ministries,** and **the same Lord.** And there are **varieties of effects,** but the*

❦

*same God who works all things in all persons. But
to each one is given the manifestation of the Spirit
for the common good...one and the same Spirit
works all these things, distributing to each one individually just as He wills.*

I Corinthians 12:4-7,11

*For just as we have many members in one body and
all the members do not have the same function, so
we, who are many, are one body in Christ, and individually members one of another. And since we
have gifts that differ according to the grace given to
us, let each exercise them accordingly...*

Romans 12:4-6

A certain unity binds Christians together, but we don't
become carbon copies of one another. The Spirit enhances our
individual roles. He helps every single person become a
productive "cell" of a healthy spiritual body which carries out
the work of Christ in the world.

When others view the living, vibrant Church, the power of
Jesus should be evident for all to see. We can't claim any credit.
Instead, His Spirit simply moves through us as we yield to Him.
Christian service of this sort reflects a wonderful partnership
where we work *with* God and not *for* Him. We trust not in human
strength alone, *for we are the true circumcision, who worship
in the Spirit of God and glory in Christ Jesus and **put no
confidence in the flesh*** (Philippians 3:3).

The verse, *...by My Spirit, says the Lord of Hosts,* reminds
us that a lifestyle of worship fills up the well-spring from which
loving, dynamic Christian service flows. No more feelings of
being driven to drudgery so we can fall asleep with clear
consciences. Rather, service bubbles out of our innermost
beings in gratitude to our precious Lord. So let's rejoice in our
union with Jesus. He is the Fountainhead of this mighty roaring

river of life. We can be confident in *His* ability to fulfill all He
has promised to do through us. Oh, what a relief!

How about if we take one last look into the heavenlies, that
the fire blazing in our hearts may intensify? But first, think back
to the chapter, "Visions of Glory," where we saw the Father
seated on His heavenly throne. We also caught a glimpse of
Jesus as both the sacrificial Lamb and the soon-coming King.
We witnessed, with the Apostle John, the countless thousands
worshipping Father and Son in the most magnificent service
ever to be assembled. The Holy Spirit wants to unveil yet one
scene in our heavenward gaze—the spectacle that will take place
at the beginning of God's judgment.

And when He broke the seventh seal, there was **silence**
in heaven for about half an hour (Revelation 8:1).

A holy hush will settle over heaven! Think of that! For the
first time since God spoke the universe into being, angelic ac-
colades will cease. No more cries of, *"Holy, holy, holy!"* ringing
forth from the throne room. No more heavenly hurrahs accom-
panying the saints' praises. An absence of sound will permeate
the universe.

Have you ever wondered what significance this moment
holds in God's plan? Thousands of years ago, He commanded
in Psalm 46:10, *"Be still and know that I am God."* In the passage
of Revelation dawns the fulfillment of this Psalm. Every being
in heaven, in earth and under the earth—even Satan—will be
silent when God the Father rises from His throne to pronounce
judgment. For one half hour, every eye will be riveted on Him
as He stands in all His unimaginable glory.

A clue to this ultimate event appears in another Psalm,
*Thou didst cause judgment to be heard from heaven; the earth
feared, and was still, when God arose to judgment, to save all
the humble of the earth* (Psalms 76:8,9).

Later, the Lord revealed to the prophet Daniel the wonders
that will follow,

> *"I kept looking, and that horn was waging war with the saints and overpowering them **until** the Ancient of Days came, and judgment was passed in favor of the saints of the Highest One, and the time arrived when the saints took possession of the kingdom."*
>
> Daniel 7:21,22

After God the Father stands, He will assume His rightful place on the throne of judgment,

> *"I kept looking until thrones were set up, and the Ancient of Days took His seat; His vesture was like white snow, and the hair of His head like pure wool, His throne was ablaze with flames, its wheels were a burning fire. A river of fire was flowing and coming out from before Him; thousands upon thousands were attending Him, and myriads upon myriads were standing before Him. The court sat, and the books were opened."*
>
> Daniel 7:9,10

Silence.

Awesome. . .deafening. . .quiet.

So great is our glorious God of heaven, that countless numbers will be speechless before Him. The Holy Spirit is working to prepare us for that day when time draws to a close. He longs to teach us to worship in reverential wonder. And yet, to worship in exuberant gratitude—with the spontaneous joy of Monarch in our opening story.

We have the opportunity of the ages. God gives us freedom to choose. How wise He is! We can run eagerly into His loving embrace. . .or turn our backs on Him. Which will it be?

❦

FIRE-SEEKER'S COMPANION
Questions for Group Interaction
or Individual Reflection

1. Karl Barth said worship is the most _____, the most _____, the most _____ action that can take place in human life. Define further each of these terms. Do they describe your attitude toward worship?

2. What happens to someone who learns to worship? Name some saints who experienced this. What is the fruit of the Spirit and how is it produced? How can you be sure *not* to produce fruit?

3. Why do you face such a struggle to worship? What will happen if the Body of Christ worships anyway? Can others see a positive difference in you? What difference should they see?

4. What can the saint give God who owns everything? Mountaintops of praise and worship enable you to get down in the valleys—and do what? Why? Service never _____ worship. Service _____ from worship.

5. Genuine service happens by what power? Who can serve God best? Do we all serve in the same way? Why or why not?

6. When will total silence fall over heaven? For how long? How will the earth respond? By contrast, what will happen to the humble?

7. Describe the scene when the Ancient of Days takes His seat. What does He look like and who is there with Him? How is God preparing you for that moment? Are you ready? Write a love letter to Him and pour out your heart.

OPEN SHARING: FEEL FREE TO DISCUSS QUESTIONS OR ANYTHING RELATED TO THE CHAPTER THAT MINISTERED TO MEMBERS OF THE GROUP. LET THE HOLY SPIRIT LEAD YOU.

FIRE-STARTER'S PREPARATION
("Lab" Exercise)

SPEND TIME ALONE AND TOGETHER WORSHIPPING THE LORD. BEFORE AND AFTER, RECORD YOUR THOUGHTS AND FEELINGS IN A JOURNAL. WRITE DOWN CHANGES YOU NOTICE IN YOUR LIFE.

NOTES

_____

_____

_____

_____

_____

_____

_____

_____

_____

_____

_____

_____

_____

_____

_____

_____

_____

_____

_____

_____

_____

APPENDIX 1

Bibliography

Holy Bible, New American Standard Version: The Lockman Foundation and Thomas Nelson Publishers, 1977.

Allen, Ronald & Borror, Gordon. *Worship - Rediscovering the Missing Jewel:* Multnomah Press, 1982.

Cornwall, Judson. *Elements of Worship:* Bridge Publishing, Inc., 1985.

Cornwall, Judson. *Let Us Worship*: Bridge Publishing, Inc., 1983.

Gibbs, Alfred P. *Worship, The Christian's Highest Occupation:* Walterick Publisher, n.d.

Jennings, Theodore W. *Life as Worship:* Wm. B. Eerdmans Publishing Co., 1982.

MacArthur, John F. *The Ultimate Priority:* Moody Press, 1983.

Mears, Henrietta C. *What the Bible is All About:* Regal, 1983.

Mumford, Bob. *Entering and Enjoying Worship:* Manna Christian Outreach, 1975.

Nee, Watchman. *The Spiritual Man:* Christian Fellowship Publishers, Inc., 1968.

Pink, Arthur W. *Profiting from the Word:* The Banner of Truth Trust, 1985.

❦

Piper, John. *Desiring God:* Multnomah Press, 1986.

Taylor, Jack R. *The Hallelujah Factor:* Broadman Press, 1983.

Tozer, A.W. *Worship: The Missing Jewel of the Evangelical Church:* Christian Publications, Inc., n.d.

Wiersbe, Warren W. *Real Worship:* Oliver Nelson, 1986.

APPENDIX 2

Notes

PART ONE

1. A.P. Gibbs, *Worship, The Christian's Highest Occupation* (Kansas City, KS: Walterick Publications, n.d.), pp. 63-64.
2. A.W. Tozer, *Worship, The Missing Jewel of the Evangelical Church* (Harrisburg, PA: Christian Publications, n.d.), p. 11.
3. Blaise Pascal, *Pascal's Pensees* trans. by W.F. Trotter (E.P. Dutton, 1958), p. 113.
4. Judson Cornwall, *Let Us Worship* (South Plainfield, NJ: Bridge Publishing, Inc., 1985), p. 11.
5. Malcolm Smith, *Rise Above Burnout* (San Antonio, TX; Malcolm Smith Ministries Teaching Cassettes, n.d.), tape 1.
6. Judson Cornwall, *The Elements of Worship* (South Plainfield, NJ: Bridge Publishing, Inc., 1983), pp. 11-12.
7. Tozer, *Worship, The Missing Jewel of the Evangelical Church*, title.
8. Cornwall, *Let Us Worship*, p. 51.
9. Tozer, *Worship, The Missing Jewel of the Evangelical Church,* pp. 7-9.
10. William Temple, *The Hope of a New World,* p. 30, cited by Allen & Borror, *Worship, Rediscovering the Missing Jewel* (Portland, OR: Multnomah Press, 1982), p. 39.
11. John F. MacArthur, *The Ultimate Priority* (Chicago: Moody Press, 1983), p. 87.
12. Tozer, *Worship, The Missing Jewel of the Evangelical Church,* p. 9.
13. Cornwall, *Let Us Worship,* p. 45.
14. John Piper, *Desiring God* (Multnomah Press, 1986), p. 65.
15. Chuck Swindoll, Message Series, "Growing Deep in the Christian Life" (Insight for Living, Fullerton, California, 1987).
16. Gibbs, *Worship, The Christian's Highest Occupation,* p. 51.

PART TWO

17. Cornwall, *Elements of Worship,* p. 199.
18. Bob Mumford, *Entering and Enjoying Worship* (Ft. Lauderdale, FL: Manna Christian Outreach, 1975), preface.
19. Gibbs, *Worship, The Christian's Highest Occupation,* pp. 157-176, 189-199.
20. Piper, *Desiring God,* p. 67.
21. MacArthur, *The Ultimate Priority,* p. 79.
22. Cornwall, *Let Us Worship,* p. 172.
23. Henrietta C. Mears, *What the Bible is All About* (Ventura, CA: Regal, 1983).
24. Cornwall, *Elements of Worship,* p. 99.
25. Theodore W. Jennings, *Life As Worship* (Grand Rapids, MI: Wm. B. Eerdmans Publishing Co., 1982), p. 65.
26. Cornwall, *Elements of Worship,* p. 82.
27. Leonard Ravenhill, *Revival Praying* (Minneapolis, MN: Bethany House Publishers, 1962), in "Last Days Magazine" (Last Days Ministries, Fall 1987), p. 26.
28. Arthur W. Pink, *Profiting from the Word* (Carlisle, PA: The Banner of Truth Trust, 1985), p. 51.
29. Ibid, p. 52.
30. Ibid, p. 49.
31. Jennings, *Life As Worship,* p. 67.

PART THREE

32. Allen & Borror, *Worship, Rediscovering the Missing Jewel,* p. 132.
33. Cornwall, *Elements of Worship,* p. 113.
34. Cornwall, *Let Us Worship,* p. 33.
35. Allen & Borror, *Worship, Rediscovering the Missing Jewel,* pp. 23-24.
36. Ibid, p. 19.
37. Ibid, p. 189.
38. Jennings, *Life As Worship,* preface.

39. Cornwall, *Elements of Worship,* p. 108.
40. MacArthur, *The Ultimate Priority,* pp. 121-122.
41. Warren Wiersbe, *Real Worship* (Nashville, Atlanta, Camden: Oliver Nelson, 1986), p. 180.
42. Gibbs, *Worship, The Christian's Highest Occupation,* p. 17.
43. Mumford, *Entering and Enjoying Worship,* p. 25.
44. Gibbs, *Worship, The Christian's Highest Occupation,* p. 216.
45. Ibid, p. 233.
46. Cornwall, *Elements of Worship,* p. 116.
47. Gibbs, *Worship, The Christian's Highest Occupation,* p. 145.
48. Tozer, *Worship, The Missing Jewel of the Evangelical Church,* pp. 5-6.
49. Cornwall, *Elements of Worship,* p. 117.
50. MacArthur, *The Ultimate Priority,* p. 155.
51. Ibid, p. 86.
52. Piper, *Desiring God,* p. 66.
53. Allen & Borror, *Worship, Rediscovering the Missing Jewel,* p. 38.
54. Tozer, *Worship, The Missing Jewel of the Evangelical Church,* p. 14.
55. Gibbs, *Worship, The Christian's Highest Occupation,* p. 199.

ABOUT THE AUTHOR

James P. Gills, M.D., is the founder and medical director of St. Luke's Cataract and Intraocular Lens Institute in Tarpon Springs, Florida. Internationally respected as a cataract surgeon, he has performed more cataract extractions and lens implantations than anyone else in the world. He has pioneered many advancements in the field of ophthalmology that make cataract surgery safer and easier for patients.

Dr. Gills has published over eighty medical papers and contributed to five books. He wrote a book about cataract extraction and lens implantation for patients, entitled, **Wonderful, Glorious Sight!** and is an active author on spiritual topics as well. He has been an avid student of the Bible for many years and has written four books about man's relationship with God. These include **Come Unto Me,** which looks at the importance of knowing God intimately; the second, **Love, What Is It?** examines commitment to God and man, while the third book of the series, **The Dynamics of Worship,** is a study of the passionate side of a Christian's inner life. **"Your Smile Is Slipping!"** takes a light-hearted look at joy. His most popular work to date, a novel co-authored with HeartLight entitled **The Unseen Essential,** has encouraged and delighted thousands of readers.

As an ultra-distance athlete, Dr. Gills has participated in a total of thirty-seven marathons, including the last nineteen of the famed Boston Marathon. He has competed in thirteen 100-mile mountain runs (he's one of only a few dozen people to complete all four major 100-mile mountain runs) and in three 200-mile runs through the rolling hills of Virginia. In addition, Dr. Gills has completed five Ironman Triathlons in Hawaii, as well as being the only person to complete five Double Ironman Triathlons in less than 30 hours. The Double Ironman consists of a 5.5-mile swim, a 224-mile bike ride and a 52.4-mile run. His passion for fitness led him, along with his son, to write **Temple Maintenance,** in which he describes the importance of physical, mental and spiritual conditioning. He received the **1990 Amateur Athlete of the Year** award.

Dr. Gills is on the Board of Trustees of Trinity College, and the national Board of Directors of the Fellowship of Christian Athletes. He is also recognized in the *Marquis Who's Who* and many other similar publications.

HOW YOU CAN HELP

Dr. Gills has provided this book at no charge via LoveLines: The Honor Innovation™. A good portion of any profits from donations to LOVE PRESS will go to the Cataract Teaching Foundation.

Founded by Dr. Gills in 1982, this non-profit organization assists and trains ophthalmologists in developing nations. Contributions help to expand the foundation's programs which provide teaching instruction and low-cost equipment to ophthalmologists, and surgery to needy people. Through a combined effort with the Christian Medical Society, CTF completed and equipped the first teaching facility in the Dominican Republic. Other developing nations view this facility as a model to follow. Each dollar Love Press gives to the Cataract Teaching Foundation will bring $10.00 worth of eyecare benefits to these nations.

P.S. News from the Heart

Coming up in mid-1992, watch for the latest release from LOVE PRESS — *Presents From Heaven: Finding Identity in a Not-So-Heavenly World,* by Dr. Tim Daley, Dr. Jim Gills and HeartLight. Their refreshing method of addressing difficult issues serves as a pleasant affirmation of God's design for every person.

Good news for those of you who enjoyed *The Unseen Essential!* The sequel promises to be even more exciting. You'll laugh and cry with Michael and Stephanie as their triumphs and trials become your own. How will Stephen fare in his battle with AIDS? Or Michelle, their teenage daughter? What's her reaction? Don't forget Sandy and his mom. Start looking for a nice, quiet niche...

Did you enjoy this LoveLines™ book?
Dr. & Mrs. James P. Gills would love to hear from you!
Please respond if this book has made an impact on you or
someone you know. Send correspondence and donations
in the postage-paid envelope provided behind this page.
God Bless You!

LOVE PRESS
St. Luke's Building
43309 U.S. 19 North ■ P. O. Box 5000
Tarpon Springs, Florida 34688-5000
Phone: (813) 938-2020, Ext. 2200
Call Toll-Free: 1-800-282-9905, Ext. 2200

LYNX PRESS